Rescuing Myself

THE STORY OF HOW I TRANSFORMED
MY BODY AFTER TURNING FORTY

NORA REYNOSO

First Printing, 2019

ISBN 978-1-7335687-2-2

Rescuing Myself
Author: Nora Reynoso
Editors: Ana Milena Varón B.
        Consuelo Quiñones C.
Translation from the Spanish: Felipe Chacon
Cover and Book Design: Felipe Castillo
Cover Picture: Jeff Hendricks II - Goliath Views

To my children,
grandchildren,
and my future generations.

"Appreciate your blessings and learn from your mistakes."

Photo by: Edward G Negron, 2018.

1.

I STARTED CRYING BUT THERE WERE NO TEARS

SUDDENLY, I felt the world was spinning around me. Everyone's words merged incoherently and I couldn't understand what they said. I didn't want to faint in front of them, I thought that if I fainted with no one around me I could recover faster. I didn't want to lose control of my body so I looked for the closest restroom. I needed a minute, just by myself, to splash my face with water and take a deep breath; then came the obvious question: What did I eat to make me feel this sick? I couldn't find an answer, at the time I didn't really want to know. I tried to find my bearings, to show the strength of a single mother of two that had everything she could ask for; to tell the world I was still the strongest and most famous bounty hunter in San Bernardino and Riverside County. So I went back, my father and sister were waiting for me to choose the color of the coffin we needed to buy.

Now, trying to recall what I had eaten around those days I can only remember the enchiladas that my mother, Abelina Reynoso, used to make. It's still one of my favorite dishes.

It was a day before my dad's 82nd birthday, when I visited my parent's house and I feasted on those enchiladas. God, they were spicy. My mom was probably mad at something. The amount of chili pepper she would use on a dish served as the perfect thermometer for her mood. You would know if she was pissed off, your tongue would feel it too. That day I was wrong, she wasn't in a bad mood, she was ill. I didn't pay too much attention to it, I finished eating and I went back to work. I had to arrest someone that hadn't shown up in court.

Maybe I should have asked myself "Why does my mom look like this? Why is she so halfhearted?" If she hadn't made dinner maybe I would've payed more attention. That would be the unmistakeable sign that something was wrong. But my own worries didn't let me see this. Besides, I was planning a party for next day.

In my house every celebration revolves around food and the most exquisite Mexican recipes are prepared by me. I don't want to blow my own horn but I am an amazing cook, I inherited that from my mother. An enormous spread would decorate the tables of my parties; It goes without saying drinks were important too. Beer, wine, a cognac here and there and some tequila always were key to my parties.

It was because of one of those parties that I couldn't attend my father's birthday. I didn't invite him that day because my mom didn't like to get out of her house. Sometimes, Doña Abelina would let me steal her husband and I would bring him to my get-togethers. She was always jealous of my guests, "Your dad's always been a flirt" she used to say.

Most, if not all, of my friends are beautiful women. They're all slim and very sensual. They had worked alongside me in promotional modeling and they later helped me promote my bail and bounty hunting business.

That day, my dad stayed at home celebrating his day, and it was the best thing he could have done. I was enjoying a nice Sunday afternoon with friends, "El Novio" as I would call my boyfriend, and my kids at home. But a call ended the joy of that reunion in one stroke, something had happened at my dad's party. I didn't get all the details, the only thing they told me is that they had found my mom laying on the floor and they were taking her to the hospital. I remember being a bit dizzy because of the beers I had drunk. But the alcohol in my blood didn't do anything to prevent the panic attack I was about to have.

At the hospital the doctors told us she had just suffered a stroke (which is an obstruction of a vein or artery caused by a blood clot). My sister told us that they were in the patio and that my mom had decided to go back in the house. Nobody knew how much time had passed until my dad found her laying on the floor.

Doña Abelina, my mother, was born on November 10th, 1932. She was always very petite, and she stood about five feet tall. She had eight children, two of them passed away. Five of her children lived in the United States and one lived in Mexico. Despite her short stature we all knew she was big. Enormous. Like a boulder you can't move or break. I don't remember her ever getting sick up until that day. She was always working, moving from one place to another, taking care of her house, her children, her husband. She was unbreakable. But then I saw her laying in her hospital bed, vulnerable, full of tubes and not being able to talk.

"This is not my mom," I thought.

Up until that moment I wasn't conscious that Doña Abelina was a seventy-eight year old woman. I'm the youngest of my siblings, and by the time my mother fell ill I was thirty-nine. I was born in Santa Monica, California and I was brought to this world when my family still had some means. Things changed quickly and soon we had to move to Inglewood, a tough town, where you either learn to defend yourself or you don't survive. At thirteen, I attended school and worked with my mom at a restaurant in Lakewood early in the morning. We gave the address of that restaurant so I could work from three in the morning and walk a short distance to school. Somehow, the school caught up with that and sent me to another school closer to home and far away from the restaurant. I preferred to keep working and I didn't go back to class. Ever. I was seventeen when I got pregnant with my first daughter and when I got married. I left home at a young age. I think that, somehow, life wanted to send me as far away from that neighborhood. I longed for safety in my life.

So I put distance between me and my family. You have to drive almost two hours to get from my house to my parents'. Even though our relationship was stable, I fought with my mom and blamed her for things in the past. There will never be a child that won't blame their parents for a painful episode in its life. Maybe we believe that they have the responsibility to help us endure all our suffering. A parent's indestructible persona might come from that belief.

That day in the hospital I realized my mother was helpless and weak. The strength she had always shown was waning. It was a struggle for her to talk and move, and she was paralyzed on her left side. The days went by and Doña Abelina pulled through. She started to recover, and I took advantage of this to ask for forgiveness, to say sorry for blaming her for my problems, to apologize for my absences and my inconsistencies. We were all happy to see her condition. My brother even built her a ramp so that she could go out to the patio and get some sun while convalescing. She was sent from the hospital to a rehabilitation facility before sending her home.

With the good news of my mom's recovery everything was going back to normal, but that didn't last. Another call came, but this one was devastating this time around. On the other end of the line a voice told me my mom had stopped breathing and had been taken to the hospital again. The voice didn't want to tell me if she had passed away but my heart felt the moment had come. As is tradition, I had to take the reins of the house, face the music, and be the one to organize my mom's funeral. Being the bearer of those news was the hardest task in my whole life. Specially because of my daughter, she loved her grandmother. I also had to give the news to my dad, tell him that the woman who he had spent almost all of his life was gone to never return.

I couldn't cry myself to sleep. I didn't let one tear out because I couldn't accept that my mother was gone, that from now on I was an orphan. Now that I think about it, I understand that I didn't take the time to accept this reality. Big mistake. Huge mistake. I also didn't think about eating, much less drinking water. The day I chose my mother's coffin I almost passed out from not having eaten all day.

I feel that everything happened too quickly, the days became hours or even minutes. In my mind this was a movie that was fast forwarding and flashing back at the same time. The confusion stopped after the burial, when we went back to my dad's place and my mother was no longer there. In that moment I decided I was going to take my dad with me. I wanted to take care of him. I thought he could very well follow on my mother's footsteps. They were married for sixty years. I don't think at any point in life he wanted to leave her. He truly loved her, despite her putting too much chile in his food every now and then.

With my dad at home I wanted to be like Doña Abelina in the kitchen, so I dedicated myself to cook a variety of recipes to please all those that would visit my home. You can bet I also kept the tradition of accompanying said meals with a few "cold ones". I also stopped going out, the only place I went was the supermarket and I managed my business form home at the time. I also made another mistake at the time, two months after my mom's passing my clothes didn't fit. I didn't give that too much thought, I thought it was a silly thing to worry about. To bid farewell to 2010 I put on some stretch pants, a big blouse and I focused on eating and drinking.

At the beginning of 2011 my daughter decided to move out of the house. She wanted a place for her and her family. It wasn't hard to accept at the time but I was going to miss my granddaughter the most, she was two years old at the time. I stayed at home with my dad, my son and my boyfriend but barely two weeks into the year my dad went back to his house. My sister was alone and she needed him. My dad left saying he couldn't come back. I understood his reasons. I ended up by myself with a teenaged son that barely visited home. I didn't want to go out of my fortress, the only thing I wanted to do was to eat and drink. I thought that by eating I was going to fill the void left by my mother's absence.

2.

I FELT THIS WAS THE END.

THERE WERE DAYS in which death and violence were a daily part of my life. I grew up listening to gang shootings, police sirens, and helicopters that skimmed the roofs of Inglewood looking for suspects. I lived the 1992 riots in Los Angeles, five days of mayhem in which the town spiraled into absolute chaos, leaving more than fifty dead and two hundred wounded. I still remember the destruction around me, and wishing to get away from it all. I needed to feel safe. I wanted to walk peacefully on the street, say hello to my neighbors and not look over my shoulder. When I had my children that wish became a necessity.

As soon as I could, I put down roots in Menifee, California, on a quiet neighborhood with a low crime rate. I worked five jobs around that time, toiling away seven days a week to pay all my bills and the house I had bought. One of those jobs was as a promotional model for Budweiser, and it was in one of those events that I was introduced to the owner of a bail bond company that wanted to open a franchise close to where I lived.

"Do you want to work for me?" He asked. "I can help you get your license," he added, showing a lot of interest in giving me a hand.

Deep inside I thought: "This guy wants something else," I can't even type, much less be able to process a bail. He gave me his business card and I waited for a week before contacting him. When we met he told me all about the business, and most importantly, the salary he was offering. With that much money I could leave three of the jobs that I had, leaving me with bail bonds and "Budweiser modeling". As with many of the opportunities I have taken in life I threw myself at it blindly. I studied, got my license, and started to make my way to the top of industry as my boss had foreseen it.

The job consists of paying the bail of the detainee and making sure that he shows up in court. You charge 10% of that to the family member or whoever is responsible. The company then fronts the rest of the total value demanded by the judge.

If the accused doesn't show up, the court takes all the money, which spells ruin for our business. Most of them comply. Some of them run. And that's why we have bounty hunters.

Those we know as "Bounty Hunters" are people that can carry weapons and have the authority to make a civil arrest, taking the accused back to jail. There's plenty of money in that industry. The owner of a bail bond company would rather pay more than 10% of the value of the bail than lose all of their money. Seeing how much you could earn doing that I took the next step and got my license to become a bounty hunter. Not long after that, I branched out and opened my own bail bond and bounty hunter company: "Nora's Angels".

It's ironic that wanting to escape from violence I would end up bailing people out of jail, and sometimes going after them. By 2011 I had nine years in the business and my boyfriend and my nephew worked with me.

Since my mom's passing, however, I didn't want to get out of the house. I don't remember going to the county jail around those days. The only thing that got me out of the house was seeing my granddaughter and having her close. I remember that, on a normal Wednesday I decided to take my little one to a Chuck E. Cheese's, a restaurant for kids with arcade games. My boyfriend wanted to come with me. He was six feet tall, strong, full of muscles, and a trained fighter. It was eleven thirty in the morning when we got there, and there weren't that many people at the restaurant. About three families by my count. We hit the arcades while we waited for our pizza.

Before lunch I wanted to go to the restroom, I asked my granddaughter if she wanted to come with me but she wanted to stay with my boyfriend. The table where we were sitting was very close to the ladies' restroom. In there, there were three stalls, the biggest one being the handicap stall. It was precisely from that stall that a man jumped out, grabbing me by the arms. I could see from his face that he was really young. I started trying to break away from his grip not understanding what was happening.

"What are you doing?" I screamed, repeatedly, while trying to break free.

Everything happened very quickly. He dragged me to the handicap stall and pinned me to the ground. As I went down, I hit the back of my head with the toilet. He immediately tried to get on top of me. At that moment I felt he wanted to kill me, that he wanted to suffocate me with his body. Every story about rape and murder that I had heard of came to mind. I tried to scream while trying to break free but I felt my screams fading into squeals in the back of my throat. He tried to cover my mouth with his hand, but because I didn't stop moving or screaming he decided to hit me. He made a fist and started punching me in the face. Quick, short hits thrown without a lot of momentum. He took his time and did it several times.

"Shut up!" He told me, while discharging all his rage in my face.

In his eyes I saw the devil. It couldn't be anything else, he looked possessed by an evil being. He was carrying a small backpack on his back and I thought he was going to pull a weapon from it. A pistol, a knife, anything he could use to murder me. In that instant he put all of his body over mine, I was almost crushed, he was a foot taller than me, but my will to live urged me to fight back, to try and defend myself. Because he couldn't subdue me he put his knees on my chest trying to suffocate me but I managed to drag myself on my back, retreating towards the wall.

"Help! Help!" I couldn't stop screaming.

Outside my boyfriend couldn't hear me, my screams were lost between the noise of the arcade and the children. He thought it was just a little girl screaming.

Since nobody answered my cries of help I thought I should try to take something from him; a DNA sample between my fingernails, a piece of his clothing, his hair, anything that could help a detective identify my rapist, and perhaps my killer too. All of that was hopeful thinking, I couldn't scratch him or take anything from him. I was trapped, up against the wall, I had no space to move, not an inch. He hit me again with even more violence and hatred than before. I ended up back on the floor where he again climbed up trying to take my clothes off. At last, the name of my boyfriend came out of my mouth.

"Carlos! ...Carlos!"

When he heard his name he knew it was me who needed help. Over the ten steps that he had to walk to reach the bathroom he might have thought that my hair was stuck on the drier or that I had slipped. He only had to open the door to see a man on top of me. Carlos, being heavier and taller, took him off of me in one move, he grabbed him by the neck and lifted him as if to strangle him with one hand. I dragged myself out to the door of the bathroom trying to breath, trying to cling on to life, I probably started crying. Carlos wanted to destroy that man but he knew it was better to immobilize him. If he harmed him we would be the ones in trouble.

My granddaughter remained outside. With only three years in this planet she came to console me. At that moment I noticed I had peed on myself but I couldn't care less. The employees of the restaurant called the cops and in the middle of the turmoil a lady that was at the restaurant with her daughters approached me.

"I'm sorry for what happened to you," She said, "I'm thankful that it was you... I was about to send my five year old to the bathroom."

The words of this woman made me understand the fragility of an assault victim; if I was trained to make an arrest, to face a situation like this, why couldn't I defend myself? What could happen to a child just like hers?

The police came and made a report, and the EMTs wanted to take me to the hospital but I refused. I just wanted to go home. I felt raped by a man that could have been my son. The irony of this attack happening in one of the safest and most quiet suburbs in the state wasn't lost on me, nothing ever happens in Menifee, and never in broad daylight. Everything I knew, what I had supposedly learned over the last forty years vanished with that attack. I always said that I was ready for an assault, and I would repeat the lesson in my mind: If you go to a dangerous neighborhood be alert, if you go to a bar where there's drunk men and it's dark outside take care of yourself. But this happened when I least expected.

Before breaking my body he took my confidence away. I got back home at around two in the afternoon. It was only then that I started feeling pain in my body. I hadn't eaten anything and I hadn't drunk a sip of water, not even to come out of shock. The first thing I did was to call my dad, because I'm the "chiquiada" of the family, daddy's girl. I wanted him to come and hug me and tell me everything would be fine. But he couldn't.

That was the day I missed my mom the most. Every time something bad happened she was always there to protect me.

"Hijo de la tiznada! If he was in front of me, I would beat him up!" Doña Abelina would've said. But she was no longer with me. I had to deal with this alone.

I called my doctor for a check up and she gave me an appointment for next day. Besides the bruises the exam revealed that in the struggle my assailant had torn one of my breasts. I think it was when he put his knees on my chest to pin me down on the ground. She gave me pain relievers and Xanax to treat anxiety, depression and panic attacks. She said I was going to feel alright. But nothing was alright. My whole organism went into disarray after the first pill, I started crying non-stop. Those were horrible days and my house was the only place I felt protected.

Next Monday I had to go into court to face my assailant. My name and my company are well known in San Bernardino and Riverside counties, I had been living in that community for 20 years. Plenty of judges, district attorneys and lawyers had heard about me. They even thought I had arrested my assailant before but it wasn't so, I had never seen this boy.

The DA told me he was barely sixteen years old, that his parents were drug addicts and that some relatives had taken him in. He also attended a school close to the restaurant. When he was arrested he said he was confused and that he had entered the ladies bathroom by accident. He said I started yelling when I saw him, that he thought I was crazy, and that he was just trying to calm me down. Besides the marks left by the struggle, the security camera revealed he had been in the bathroom for fifteen minutes waiting for his victim.

When I heard his story I began seeing him in a different light, so human, so helpless. I even entertained the thought that my assailant could have been a victim. Maybe someone abused him when he was a child.

His family came to tell me how sorry they were, and that he had been through a lot. I felt awful at that moment. I was thinking of dropping the charges but my boyfriend brought me back to earth in an instant.

"Stop thinking about everyone else, think for yourself for once."

His words still resonate to this day. Back in court I left my maternal instinct behind, the one that makes me want to care for everyone, and I tried to be rational. I analyzed the moment of the attack. I understood this young man was a sexual predator, that he had planned the assault and that he would surely do it again. Unfortunately, time would prove me right. Because my assailant was a minor and this was his first offcnsc thc judgc was lenient and sentenced him to thirty days in jail. He didn't even have to register as a sex offender. He was free after thirty days while I couldn't get out of the house.

3.

SUDDENLY... I GAINED WEIGHT.

A FTER THE ATTACK I spent several days doing nothing. All of a sudden I found myself sitting in bed or on the couch all alone. I didn't want to speak with anybody. Boredom became my new best friend until I reached a point where I had to say to myself:

"Nora, you can't keep doing this!"

I decided to get back into my routine, to take care of my children, my house and my business. But always from home of course

When I think about it, I reckon this was my biggest problem. I never gave myself the time, or even take the necessary steps, to recover from the blows life had given me. I tried in vain to eliminate the last six months of my life in the same way you try to remove a stain but end up throwing the piece of clothing away instead. What I didn't know is that this stain had seeped through the fabric and had reached deep into my soul.

The days went by, and then the months went by, and then my life went back to normal. Although, I would only go out of the house if I really had to. After getting tired by this routine I decided to treat myself to a trip for my 40th birthday. My younger years were going away and it was time to do the things I always wanted to do. It was my opportunity to escape with my boyfriend and enjoy a romantic week in a tropical paradise. What all girls dream of when we are younger. But a call came threatening to ruin all my plans. The prosecutor that had accused my attacker wanted to speak to me. As soon as I heard his voice on the other side of the line I remember the prophecy I made the day we were in court. My inner voice told me:

"He did it again. He attacked someone else."

Only a few seconds went by before the prosecutor confirmed my fears.

"We need you to testify again. The other victim is scared and doesn't want to come forward."

It hadn't been six months since he had tried to rape me. For his second attack he chose an apartment complex he had lived in a few months back. He crouched hiding in a children's park waiting for a young mother to walk by him. This time the victim was carrying her youngest son while holding the oldest by the hand. The prosecutor told me that as soon as she passed him by he pushed her, sending her and her two children to the ground. As it happened in my case, in his desperation to abuse this woman he couldn't immobilize her. She screamed for help and her husband came to her rescue. If you think about how this guy operates we can safely assume he is a sexual deviant. Only that explains an attack in broad daylight.

The second victim didn't want to testify against him. She argued that she was afraid he would assault her again. The prosecutor wanted me to testify hoping this would give her confidence. Remembering that episode was not something I wanted to do, but I thought it was nobler to give courage to this young mother and help them stop this guy. So I decided to testify again. Fortunately the audience wouldn't be until February of next year (2012) so I could still make that trip and celebrate I was still alive.

I dropped everything for two weeks and travelled with my boyfriend to Costa Rica. The first few days we explored all the exotic places that country had to offer. We walked, we ate, and we drank until we couldn't do it anymore. On the second week we stayed at an all-included resort and everything was beyond perfect. There were endless buffets with any type of food you can imagine. Meat, shrimp, beans, plantains, salads, were all part of a menu that I would never finish. And let's not even mention the drinks, we had a private bar in my room, and there were 24-hour bars around the hotel you could visit. Beer, ron de caña, and a whiskey or two were transforming that place into my kind of paradise.

The day after we arrived to the hotel we were in the pool laughing and drinking with other tourists. The sun was going down and me and my boyfriend wanted to go somewhere more intimate. We dreamt of watching the sunset while holding hands on the beach and kiss in front of the sea and this seemed like the perfect time.

I was wearing one of my bikinis. I had been wearing them since very young and I learned how to rock a two piece very well. I had always been petite, skinny, "curiosita" as they would say in my house. In my youth I learned how to accentuate my body, and even though it was't perfect it was harmonious. If I put on some heels I would transform into a total bombshell, as my friends would say. I worked for many years as a Budweiser girl thanks to that. That day, as I was walking towards the beach, I felt like that girl who decades before would leave men with their mouths gaping. With my boyfriend by my side, a handsome man standing more than six feet tall, we looked like the perfect couple. And you could tell we were really in love.

When we got to the beach there was a hotel worker, who very kindly handed us a beach towel. In the exact moment he handed me a towel he smiled from ear to ear and told me with gusto: "Congratulations!"

I was amused, I didn't know why the towel man was congratulating me. My boyfriend was puzzled, he spoke very little Spanish and didn't even understand what was happening.

Curious, I asked him why he was congratulating me, to which he pointed at my belly and added:

"Congratulations... On the baby!"

Baffled, I looked down and saw what was evident to everyone but me: The extra pounds that made me look pregnant. My boyfriend quickly figured out what was said and wanted to kill the poor man. For him this was an insult. How dare he say that to his queen? To the most perfect woman in the world?

"I'm going to kick his ass," He said, his gaze jumping back and forth between my potbelly and the towel man.

I reacted quickly and grabbed his hand. I took him closer to the water and told him everything had been a misunderstanding, that everything was fine. The towel man had been left behind not knowing what to do. He was surely not smiling now. When I relive that scene I remember my boyfriend telling me that the worker wanted to ruin our moment and me answering "Fat chance". A poor choice of words for the occasion.

We continued walking on the beach to see the sunset. I spent the rest of the afternoon blaming the "inflammation" in my tummy, my hips, my legs, my arms and my whole body on the amount of liquor we had drunk. I also had to recognize I was about to turn forty.

"It must be my age," I told myself.

Maybe life was sending me a message with this man, that it was time to wear a one piece bikini from now on. Maybe I was old and the Nora that promoted Budweiser was now in the rearview mirror. Even though I wasn't too far from the truth, I wasn't really aware of what was happening to me.

Ready to leave that embarrassing episode behind we finally went to watch the sunset and then went out for dinner and drinks. We returned home five days later. Now, if I thought I looked overweight before my vacation, I was "triple-overweight" when I came back. I had put on fifteen pounds! I think if towel man had seen me land back in California he would have thought I was giving birth to octuplets.

Back at home I forgot all about it and focused on getting ready for the holidays. The second time we celebrated them without my mom. Like every other Christmas since we moved to Menifee, I planned a party with Puerto Rican food, my children's favorite. I made roast pork, which I had left marinating a day before. On the menu, gandule rice, cheese balls, and dressed artichokes accompanied the main course. For dessert we had rice pudding and pumpkin pie. The Mexican touch was present in the drinks. I made spiked fruit punch. At the bar, the adults could enjoy beer, wine and champagne for the toast.

I started cooking and cleaning the house in the morning. At six in the afternoon everything almost was ready to be served so I decided it was time for me to doll up. I have a walking closet in my room, I'm tidy, and every piece of clothing is classified and organized to make it easier to find what I want to wear.

I have always said that one of my great qualities was learning how to dress to enhance my attributes. Everything is an optical illusion, so I concealed the unflattering parts and highlighted the good ones. Once you learn that lesson it isn't hard to dress for every occasion. But that day proved me wrong, I started trying blouses and I soon found out none of them fit me anymore so I moved on to pants and skirts. I like clothes that are elastic and stick to your body but that afternoon the elastic wasn't giving up. Everything was uncomfortably tight or didn't even fit at all.

Earlier, I felt my glutes were bigger when I was in the shower, same with my legs. I have implants in my chest, they're big and they wouldn't let me see my tummy very well. It never crossed my mind that my body was out of control and I was gaining weight. The towel man had seen it weeks before but I couldn't understand how evident this was.

With every blouse, shirt, and pair of pants on the floor I started crying. In the beginning those were tears of helplessness, of not being able to understand what had happened to that skinny girl who could wear almost anything. It didn't take much for the dam to break and I cried even harder, whimpering every now and then. In that moment my boyfriend came and asked me if I was okay while trying to make sense of the mess on the floor.

"Nothing fits anymore." I told him, wiping the tears off my face.

"Don't worry, you're beautiful, you know I love you." He said while hugging me.

Instead of feeling reassured, I cried harder instead. I wanted to throw him out the window for what he told me. In that moment what I heard was: "Don't worry, I'll love you even if you're fat." I wanted him to lie to me, to say:

"Nora, you're crazy, you're not fat."

As plenty of people in the world do I decided to ignore my problem. I washed my face and I put on the biggest blouse I had with the one elastic pant that did fit me. Jewelry and make-up made me realize that there was still beauty in my exterior. The tantrum had been left behind, and at the end of the day whatever happened to my body didn't matter. I had a partner that thought I was the most beautiful woman in the world. My children were proud of their mom. Everything was going to be fine.

Christmas Eve arrived. As usual, the party was phenomenal, there was food aplenty and the drinks, with and without alcohol, were abundant. Among the guests was my friend Guadalupe Moreno, known to me as Lupita "La was bonita" (the prettiest one). We had known each other for fifteen years and helped me promote my business as part of "Nora's Angels". Even though she was also a grandmother like myself nobody saw Lupita with those eyes. She was fit, she was gorgeous, she was 120 pounds of dynamite in a 5'5" frame. She practiced sports and she was into bodybuilding. She had a healthy diet and she never drank alcohol. And beyond her figure she was also a wonderful person. Cool, kind, the type of friend that will always be by your side and will always have your back. Beautiful inside and out.

Halfway through the party, the decadence of my scene at the closet was forgotten. The drinks were of great help in that regard. I was making myself a Margarita when Lupita approached me and asked me without hesitation:

"Why don't you try bodybuilding?"

"Mija, come on. That's not for me." I answered.

4.

THE CHALLENGE OF A NATURAL TRANSFORMATION

ALMOST A YEAR after my rape attempt I had to face my assailant again. He looked more mature, I even thought he had grown up. The only thing that hadn't changed was the expression of his face, he still looked like a scared child. He was feigning innocence, as if he hadn't done anything. The prosecutor wanted to use my testimony to convince the judge that this young man was a real danger but he strategy didn't work. His punishment was light, and he was sentenced to a few months of jail. I came out of the court disappointed and distressed for having to remember the assault.

To leave this dreadful feeling aside, I decided to accompany Lupita do Zumba. Dancing seemed to be the perfect cure. The problem was that I couldn't move as I did before, the extra pounds had wrecked my body. My back, my legs and even the tip of my toes ached. There were moments in which I couldn't move, afraid of the pain I felt.

My mom would have sent me to the "sobandero" right away, but since she wasn't by my side anymore I had to go to the doctor. After a five minute consult the doctor told me that my sciatic nerve was inflamed. The only options to fight the pain were pills and several visits to the chiropractor. I don't remember him ever telling me that my weight was making this worse.

The pain made me run to the chiropractor, so much so that I had to ask for an appointment right away. As my luck would have it, my chiropractor was absolutely handsome and I had to go twice a week to see him. But the visits reminded me that my age was showing. I was used to men flirting with me, undressing me with a simple look. This time was different, I was just a patient for him, maybe one that he didn't want to see that often.

He suggested I exercise to make the pain disappear and I followed his recommendation, although without consistency. With the little exercise I was doing while dancing I gained back some mobility and I was even breathing better, but my weight didn't change. I did feel a major change in my mood, however. I felt happier, almost as I used to feel before the death of my mom. By then, I discovered that exercise helps your body, and your brain in particular, produce endorphins. This substance is responsible for pleasant feelings, and it helps easing pain.

Lupita would accompany me to my dance lessons. Always by my side, like the unconditional friend she has always been. I think that, having seen my change in attitude, she decided to take the next step. One day, she came with this crazy idea that we had to transform ourselves, and that she knew a coach who promised changes in just a few weeks. Lupita didn't have anything to change though, she was perfect! She had just won a bodybuilding contest. You can deduce that, if she didn't need to change, she was doing this for me. I must have looked wretched at the time. To thank her for this kind gesture we went to meet the coach, but I have to confess that when I saw the place I was a little disappointed. It wasn't a gym, rather, it looked like a wine cellar with a boxing ring and some weights thrown around. To be fair, I had done my research and the place had very good reviews. The coach was a businesswoman, she was concise and I liked that. As soon as we stepped in she made us try on a bikini to see how bad the situation was.

In that moment I could only think: Good god, again with the bikini!

I immediately remembered the mishap in Costa Rica, and my "brief" pregnancy. This time, however, was much worse because I was standing next to Lupita. She had her "six pack" and I was rocking a keg. I began to think this was a horror movie, but we were already there and I wasn't going to sound the retreat. Her method consisted of a strict diet, and an extensive workout. After being examined in the bikini she gave us a quote. Obviously, mine was a little heftier than my friend's. I don't even understand why she would charge Lupita, but business is business. In 2012 the "natural transformation" wasn't as popular as it is now so my wallet took a big hit. I also decided to pay for my friend's transformation. It was the least I could do, the solidarity she had shown to me had no price. We began the routine that very day under the promise that it would make us fit and beautiful.

The challenge began with the workout. We had to go to the gym for one hour every day from Monday to Saturday, preferably in the morning, and then do another hour and a half of exercises in the evening. On the nutrition front, we had to eat six times a day every three hours. At first I thought this couldn't be a diet, but when she mentioned what we could eat, and the size of the portions I understood that I wasn't going to even smell a good part of the food that I liked. Red meat was forbidden. We were only allowed to have four to six ounces of fish or chicken a day, accompanied by green vegetables, preferably asparagus; a quarter cup of rice or oats per day was allowed as well. To top it all I had to stop eating bread, carbohydrates, and therefore all my favorite Mexican dishes. We had to drink one gallon of water a day without excuse. This was the only drink allowed. I couldn't drink aguas frescas, sodas, any sugary drinks or any type of liquor. The latter was one of the hardest things to accomplish: What would happen with the "cervecitas" I was used to?

The goal was to consume 1,400 calories a day. At first I didn't understand this topic very well and why it was so important for my health. I had never done a diet in my life. On the contrary, there was a time in my life when I ate in excess hoping some parts of my body would finally develop; but that was a long time ago. I began my transformation with determination. At first the workouts were taking its toll but the universe seemed to give me a hand with the diet it. My daughter and granddaughter weren't living with me, my son was always at school and my boyfriend got a job that was keeping him busy so I had the kitchen to myself. I had to control myself and avoid the temptation of eating of bread or cheese, I needed to get off my mind the thoughts of gummy bears, a personal weakness. Fruit, which I loved, was also restricted to only five blackberries a day. Can you imagine that? I could drink coffee or tea but without milk. Sugar was forbidden, I could only use honey or certain sweeteners.

I can't say that eating baked fish and asparagus every day is easy. By the fifth day you won't even want to smell it. During the first week, the diet became a big sacrifice, I was famished, but whenever I thought about giving up I said to myself:

"Nora, if you can't control what you eat, how can you even want to have control other aspects of your life?"

This mantra wasn't enough. I believe that my error was not preparing my mind so that I could make this easier on my body. I thought I was hungry all the time and I began to feel anxious.

Obviously, the change was abrupt, and even though I was doing something good for my body, my body couldn't understand it. I should have had a serious talk with myself to make my body understand that this was good for my health.

After a week the anxiety faded away. My organism was getting used to this routine and I was feeling lighter, I can even say that my body felt happy. I could hear my body saying: "Thank you". Although I wasn't pleased by the diet, I began to love all the cardio exercises. My body felt it could run or ride a bike. I could also move my neck and my back was straightening up again.

Along with the aerobic exercises I began to do weight training. This routine was split into two: One day I worked the upper part of my body (My chest, back and arms) and the following day I devoted myself to the lower part (My legs and hips). The routine was always twenty minutes for every exercise. Little by little I began to like my time in the gym, it felt like an oasis in the middle of a desert. In addition to the physical change, the exercise helped me change my state of mind. I felt as if the true Nora emerging, as if I was finally discovering the woman hiding deep inside.

After six weeks of following the routine to a "T" I had lost thirty pounds.

I DID IT!

The pain of my mother's passing was still present but now it was bearable, and the panic attacks caused by my rape attempt were disappearing. A bigger challenge was now on the horizon. Having seen the good results of training and dieting, our coach suggested we enter a famous amateur bodybuilding contest in Venice Beach. The same one that made Arnold Schwarzenegger famous. I didn't think it twice, I said: Yes!

Another adventure had begun.

5.

MY NEW ADVENTURE

THE POSSIBILITIES of gaining back weight after such a strict diet, like the one I did, were very high. Trainers have a term for this: "Rebound". If you don't change your eating habits or continue with your exercise routine those pounds will be back. Against this background, the best thing that could have happened to me was to enroll in this competition. I qualified for two categories: "Bikini Open," in which women of all ages compete against each other, and "Master Bikini," for women thirty-five and older. Yes, bikinis are a recurrent theme in my life. In this category they evaluate a toned body, so a woman doesn't need to have totally defined muscles. And even though I thought I was going to land in last place I wanted to leave a good impression. I maintained my exercise routine and diet. The only thing I had to change was my water consumption. Bodybuilders try to drain the body, literally.

My kids and my boyfriend were supporting me in this new adventure. They were excited that I was going to compete in the same place where Schwarzenegger and Lou Ferrigno (The Incredible Hulk) became household names. They told me over and over that it could be the first step for a career in television, they wanted to encourage me. My friend Lupita, who had participated in this type of competition before, became my guide. She taught me the exercises I needed to do to accentuate my muscles and burn the residual fat that was in my body. This new regime didn't bother my boyfriend at all, all the opposite, he even went to the gym with me from time to time. He was getting bored with the diet though. Our passion for food and drinks had been crucial early in our relationship, it was our bond. Going out to dinner or for a beer was a habit. But since I started my diet and my new training regimen those plans were off the table.

When the day came, my body looked healthier. The targeted workout had built my muscles, I could see it right away on my glutes, my legs, and my belly. The competition was going to take place on Memorial Day and we had to register at five in the morning; after registering we would have to retouch our tans. Bodybuilders have to put on make up in their whole body to make it pop when they are on the runway. Putting some color on your skin highlights the muscles in all their splendor. For me, this process is art. Everything is crucial, from picking the color, to how shiny you want it to be. I had to tan the day before and retouch it minutes before the competition.

With all this in mind I chose to leave a day before, and booked two rooms in a hotel in Venice Beach. We arrived, quite excited, with my son, a friend he invited and my boyfriend. I escaped for a few hours to work on my tan. When I came back to my hotel my boyfriend told me he wanted to go eat and drink, and seemed to have had a couple of beers while he waited for me. My only wish for that night was to rest. I was tired from running around all day and I had to wake up really early for registration. Besides I couldn't drink anything. My negative was like a bucket of cold water for Carlos, he always had a girlfriend who would say yes to every request. He recriminated me saying that he wouldn't share dinner with me.

My boyfriend liked the result of the diet and what exercise had done to my body, but what he didn't like was the impact this was having on our day to day lives. We were no longer the compadres that went drinking together. Now that I think about it, did my boyfriend think that the best way of supporting me before a competition where my stomach had to be flat was an invitation for food and drinks? In that moment, the Nora that came out was the one that always pleased everyone, the one that dropped everything she was doing to help someone else with their dreams. With a tan that was still setting in my body and an empty stomach I asked him:

"Do you want to go home?" It wasn't sarcasm. This was defeat.

The answer never came out of his mouth. Before our argument kept escalating I went to the bathroom. I was there for a while, looking at myself in the mirror, upset with what had happened. I stopped and I saw in that reflection the Nora I liked, the fighter, the one that doesn't crumble when adversity shows up. I decided this was not the time to give up. I knew that this wasn't the biggest contest but I had put a lot of effort to get there. I had followed a strict diet and I had done a grueling workout for hours on end. More than once I wanted to drop the weights and go home but I had achieved getting to 108 pounds. If I withstood all that pain, if I didn't give up when I was tired, why would I have to quit now?

It wasn't the first time that I got into trouble out of love. Years back, when we went to live at Menifee with the father of my children I decided to get five jobs so that my husband could go back to school. I hadn't finished my high school and I thought I wasn't smart enough to get a degree and a career. So I decided to sacrifice myself so that he could follow his dream. I was always like the faithful soldier marching blindly into the line of fire. The problem wasn't that I had decided to postpone my studies to support him economically. The problem appeared when he unloaded the responsibility of the home on my shoulders. To make things worse, he decided to drop out, and I didn't scold him. In that moment, I didn't understand that love does not require sacrificing my dreams. After a few minutes of introspection, of traveling back to the past to look at the mistakes I had made, I went out to tell my boyfriend that if he wanted to go back he could do so by himself.

When I opened up the door, full of rage, I saw Carlos sleeping. I slept right by his side still mad at him. The next morning I woke up early ready to have some fun. I never thought that contest would change my life forever.

Training

Our body is our temple, and we must treat it with respect.

Personal album, 2014.

6.

A NEW WORLD

RUNWAYS DON'T SCARE ME. I learned to walk with grace and poise when I did promotional modeling. I can walk on heels since I was a teenager. Wearing a bikini wasn't too hard either, not even when I was so fat I looked pregnant. Those were the advantages I arrived with to my first bodybuilding contest.

In my first contest I felt that the years weighed on me, I was competing against twenty other women of all ages. Some were barely eighteen. Obviously, I was one of the older ones. And as the contest started so did the presentation of my muscles. And yes, that's what those contests are all about, who's got the best muscles. To be honest, I had never stopped to think how, with proper exercise, the tissue that is responsible for movement is formed.

Like in beauty pageants, five finalists are chosen from all the contestants, but I already felt I had won something. I was happy to regain my body, and at looking better than I did when

I was young. All of a sudden the name Nora Reynoso was along the five finalists. I couldn't believe it. I don't remember if I was fourth or fifth at the end of the contest but I do remember I did not finish in the top three. At that moment I didn't care, I was so proud of myself, of having gone that far, that I felt I had taken the first place.

Still euphoric, I participated in the competition of Master Bikini. The number of contestants was almost the same, but this time my rivals were thirty-five years and older. I thought I was facing a fairer competition for my age at the time. The routine was the same, the only difference was that when the jury selected me in the five finalists again more adrenaline and emotion rushed through my body. I had exceeded all expectations, and I was happy with these achievements. Even though winning against fifteen women seems a banal triumph, I felt that the confidence I had lost after so many defeats in life was coming back. I understood I had the power to choose what I could eat. The pride I felt rose and rose when I kept hearing my name. Now I was in the top three finalists. I can still hear the applause and the screams from the audience in my head, it still gives me goosebumps. I ended up third, and I received a prize for taking care of my body.

Everyone was jubilant so we decided to celebrate at a restaurant. Ironic, I know. I ate nachos and I accompanied them with a cocktail. But I shouldn't have eaten that, because it was like a kick to my stomach. That was my body's way of warning me that I should take things slowly and that you can't play with your body. As always, I learned that lesson late. I think it was life's way of keeping me on the path of caring for my body and my spirit. I went back home with my achievements.

Not long after, when I went to say goodbye to the trainer I thought that this would be the end of this adventure. But before I opened my mouth she suggested I should keep competing, that if I trained for six more weeks to perfect my form I would arrive better prepared to the next competition. Strategy was always part of her business. So after a week of not dieting I restricted my food intake once more and I came back to the six meals a day plan. My purpose was to compete in the amateur league of the Professional Natural Bodybuilding Association (PNBA/INBA). In this league you can't take pills or supplements to drop weight or gain muscle.

Carlos was very loving around that time, he knew he had done something wrong at the hotel. He loved how good I looked, and now his girlfriend was not only the owner of a bail bond company but she was also a woman admired because of her body and her persistence. Six months went by and life seemed to have gone back to normal. Even though the pain of losing my mom was still in my heart, exercise and the challenges that bodybuilding brought me made me realize I couldn't give up. My mom wouldn't have liked to see me throw in the towel.

My boyfriend loved to see the Nora of old, or an improved version of her. And he responded by trying to be the perfect man, making sure to be by my side at every project. We would meditate and do exercise, and we would no longer need alcohol to feel happy. I competed again and this time I took first place in my division. I also participated in other categories where I swept the competition. Among my prizes I found my credentials to turn into a professional bodybuilder.

I didn't believe that this was happening to me at age forty. Here I was, a grandmother and a woman who had her fair share of stumbles in life about to become a professional in something. I was on cloud nine and I stayed there for a good while. Even the owner of the organization, Denny Kakos, acknowledged my hot streak:

"You look amazing, keep it up."

His words stayed with me and assured me I was on the right path. I decided to take this opportunity and start my life over. A lot of people started to call me asking how I had managed to transform my body at the same time I managed my business. People even said I inspired them, which I thought incredible. Nora, the girl from Inglewood, had become a role model. My mother would have been proud.

7.

LA JEFA.

IN THE MIDDLE of my honeymoon with bodybuilding came another opportunity. My company's car had a picture of me and Nora's Angels, and my boyfriend happened to be driving around Dodger Stadium when a television producer asked him about my business. After Carlos told him the whole deal, the man showed interested and told him he would get in touch with us to talk about pitching a television series. Initially I didn't pay that much attention but a few days later the producer called and we arranged a meeting. He wanted to make a reality show. The idea was to tell the story of a suspect escaping, getting chased and then getting arrested in each episode

Everyone working in my bail bond company was thrilled by this idea. My boyfriend and I would be the protagonists. My daughter, her boyfriend and my nephew, who were working for me, would complete the cast. The project took off immediately. In less than two months we were shooting the pilot, and my boyfriend's father lent us his house to shoot some scenes. His home was very pretty and it had a lot of space for us to shoot.

My company had been around for ten years by then, and I had been working in the industry for twelve. You could tell I was experienced. I was the brains of the operation, I mean, there was a reason it was Nora's Angels. Nobody doubted I was the one in charge, but what I hadn't realized was how obvious it was.

The producer and the director wanted to capture the realism of one of our arrests and we tried to act naturally. But the truth is that most of the people that are arrested and are released on bail actually make their court date, the money fronted to the client is recovered and we even turn a profit. There's always one or two that don't show up to court. Some of them get scared because they face a long sentence, so they decide to run and become fugitives. The producers made it clear they were only interested in those cases.

Planning those arrests doesn't take that much time, they have to be done quickly to prevent the suspect from fleeing to another state or even outside of the country. Generally, the person that hired the bail bondsman has put its house as collateral and is usually the one that tips us with information about the location of the suspect. These operatives are called civic arrests and bounty hunters have the authority to detain these fugitives and take them back to jail. We're armed, and even though the idea is to make the arrest without a shot, we are trained to do it.

I knew this was a dangerous business from the get go. However, it wasn't until I had to make an arrest by myself that I understood the risk we faced. It was a Sunday and I had gotten a tip about the location of a young fugitive charged with a drug related crime. The relative of the young fugitive called me to give me the information, and I told him to meet me in a corner close to his hideout. Before that I tried contacting my teammates for backup but they were all busy, or too far away to come in time. I knew that if I didn't detain this guy I would lose a lot of money, so I didn't have a choice. The neighborhood where he was hiding was known to be full of gangs and drugs. When Ignacio, the relative that called, saw me arrive by myself he was surpriscd. I didn't lct him brcathc, I couldn't lct him gct scared, I needed him as my backup.

"Lets go," I told him as I walked past him.

After a few minutes we entered a crummy building. The apartment was located on the second floor, and Ignacio hid behind me while I knocked on the door. A young man opened but he wasn't the one I was looking for. When I asked for the fugitive the young guy talked back to me, told me he wasn't there and tried to shut the door. I stuck my foot in quickly preventing him from closing the door, opened it up with both hands and got in. Ignacio was right behind me trembling. There was another boy in the living room, and he got scared the moment he saw my gun. I closed the door and barked at them:

"Tell him to get out, I know he's here."

"I told you he's not here." The boy that opened the door replied.

"Then I'm staying until he comes back."

One of the rooms had the door closed. I asked:

"Who's in there?"

"Nobody!" He said.

You see, I knew they were lying to me, so I opened the door anyway. I found a third man in the room, he was sleeping. I caught a glance but he wasn't who I was looking for. The kid didn't even realize I was in his room, the drugs had him in a stupor. I went back to the living room and asked for the boss.

They looked at each other, they didn't understand what was happening. How did I know who was in charge? I grabbed a cellphone I found on top of a table and ordered one of them to call him. In the beginning they didn't even touch the phone, my hand was still stretched pushing them to do it. While this was happening Ignacio was on a corner, pale, and looking like he was about to pass out. The boy that opened the door took the phone form my hand, made the call and when someone answered him I took the phone back.

"I'm looking for one of your clients. He hasn't shown up in court, I know he's one of your boys but I just want him to come with me." I told the boss.

Without missing a beat I continued.

"If I don't find him I'm bringing the cops and whoever I happen to find."

On the other side of the line, the boss of these guys answered calmly,

"Give me two hours and come back for him."

I hung up and when I gave the phone back I threatened them:

"I'll be back in two hours."

Before I left I took several pictures of the drugs they had and their faces. I was pissed off, behind me was Ignacio, who was so pale he was almost transparent. When I came down the stairs I felt my knees buckle but I had to keep a straight face. When I got to my car I told Ignacio:

"Don't worry, I'll come for him in two hours."

I got in my car, turned on the engine and left to look for someone to back me up.

Every time I remember this moment I wonder: What would have happened if any of those guys had taken my gun? Or if their boss had arrived? What if they had been armed and decided to shoot me? I always do the sign of the cross when I remember this moment and thank god because nothing happened to me. I promised myself I wouldn't put myself at risk like this ever again. Two hours later I was back with one of my guys and the outlaw was there. He didn't resist the arrest when we took him, and he didn't try to escape when we returned him to jail.

These were the kind of stories that the producers were looking for, something that could capture the audience. The problem was that we weren't chasing fugitives every day. For the pilot we had to improvise and we made up a case involving a fugitive. When we started taping the show the camera showed that the shortest person in the room was the one in charge. I was the one giving orders, I ran the operation the way I wanted and everyone obeyed me.

One day, we started watching what we just had shot. I remember my father in law being there. The images didn't lie, they showed that in that company, in that relationship, I was the one holding the reins, and Carlos's world revolved around me. I felt awkward. But, I knew that my boyfriend had fallen in love with the strong woman, the heroin that went after the bad guys. It was in that moment I realized my boyfriend was seventeen years younger than me. He was twenty-five, I was about to turn forty-two.

8.

BLINDSIDED

THE FIRST DAY I saw Carlos I thought he was a very manly and handsome man. His height, his body, and his lovely big eyes helped me fall in love with him despite him being younger than me. After getting to know him I found out he was kindhearted, with genuine and honest feelings. He was also very mature for his age. With time I realized that the most important thing was that he really loved me. I could honestly say I felt loved.

Carlos became the perfect couple, he would help me with my kids, with my business, and with my expenses when he didn't have that much money. When we started living together he barely earned $1,000 every two weeks. At that time all the expenses of the house averaged $10,000. He was practically giving me all his paycheck. And even though I had to answer for 80% of the expenses I was happy.

Carlos' parents knew me and they accepted our relationship. And even though my mom preferred me having a more adult person she also gave him her blessing. My kids loved him and they got along very well with him. My friends welcomed him to the group. All in all, everyone loved Carlos.

The only obstacle between us was his wish to have kids and me not being able to have them anymore. But the matter was forgotten quickly and we started becoming a very happy couple. We were meant for each other. So much so, that you wouldn't notice the age difference. It looked like he would take years off of me, making me younger, and I would make him look more mature.

In the middle of October the producers had finished taping the pilot and we had to wait for a couple of months to see if someone was interested in buying it. And because we didn't depend economically from this opportunity our life just went back to normal.

December arrived and it was time to celebrate my birthday. This time I only invited six of my closest friends. I remember it was a Sunday and people arrived early. I prepared dinner and because I was still training and exercising I wasn't drinking any liquor, so alcohol was off-limits at the party.

After dinner and a small toast I opened my gifts. Carlos had given me a card that was very pretty. I read it aloud for everyone to hear:

"I will love you always. If you are ever in doubt, look at your star and I will be there."

When I finished reading it my eyes were misty. My friends were melting because of the romance in those words. I kissed him and thanked him.

By 8:00 in the evening everyone had left, which was strange if we compared it to past celebrations. We did the dishes and then we went back to the room. I put my pajamas on, he was still wearing his normal clothes when all of a sudden he said:

"We need to talk"

I sat in bed with a strange feeling. I wouldn't know how to describe it, I didn't understand what was happening.

"I have to go," He continued.

I was still confused, I didn't understand what he was talking about.

"Where are you going?" I told him.

I thought he wanted to leave because he had to work early next day but it wasn't so. He just kept repeating that he had to go. I was perplexed, lost. He took advantage of my silence to take a breath and deliver the final stroke. Without looking at me he continued:

"I've had time to reflect and I just realized that I'm living in your world and not in mine."

I don't know how much time it took him to tell me all of this, maybe was even less than a second, or maybe it was an eternity. I just stood there with my jaw on the floor, listening while he kept talking, rationalizing his decision:

"I realized that I want to have a family. I love you very much but I have to go."

I remember barely stammering something.

"We haven't had a fight. Why are you leaving?"

There wasn't anything to be done, Carlos had decided to end our relationship. His last words before he left knocked the air out of me.

"I'm not taking anything with me."

I only managed to mumble: "Don't leave."

But he walked out of the room without looking at me. I was left sitting in a corner of my bed. There was something inside of me hoping that this was a prank, that Carlos would come back, that this was just a cruel joke.

The seconds turned into minutes, the minutes into hours. Tears poured out of me but I didn't feel I was crying. I was paralyzed with fear, I couldn't believe this was happening. The man of my life, my husband, my boyfriend, my everything, was gone.

9.

THE PHANTOM PAIN

I SPENT THE WHOLE NIGHT AWAKE. Sunlight came in through my window and I hadn't moved. I was stunned, speechless. It seems my body decided to go on auto-pilot because I got up from bed as if nothing had happcncd. Thc night Carlos left for good my kids were asleep. It was such a quiet exit that nobody noticed his absence. I don't remember what I did that day, it must have been a Monday like any other. My son went to school, my daughter went to work and my granddaughter was with her dad. This meant I was alone. Everyone thought Carlos was working and that I was dealing with company errands. Nobody payed any attention to me. They didn't stop to see that I was looking for the man I had lost, the man that had left me the night before. Or maybe my kids didn't ignore my suffering but it was me who decided to avoid them, locking myself up in the bathroom and letting the shower run. That was always comforting.

Four days went by like this. Nobody knew what happened to Carlos and I don't even think I understood the situation. I don't remember anything about what happened in those ninety-six hours of my life. It's as if time had gone with him. I only have memories of a feeling in my chest and an emptiness in my body. That feeling didn't let me eat, didn't let me drink a glass of water, and worst of all, didn't let me sleep.

On the third day I was talking over the phone with a client that was making t-shirts for me to promote my business and he realized something wasn't right. I'm very calm, I don't scream or even raise my voice. I also try to be kind with everyone that works with me, I like people saying I'm cool to work with. That day was different.

In the middle of the conversation the client interrupted me:

"Calm down! What's wrong with you?" He asked.

I was talking at a hundred miles an hour and I was screaming too. I had lost all control over my emotions. Trying to calm down I hung up the phone. Seconds later my mind was blank and I couldn't remember what I did for the rest of the day. The day after was different, it was December 19th, and to date I haven't been able to forget that day.

My day began taking my son and one of his friends to a church in Temecula, I picked them up in the afternoon and we all went home. Everything seemed to be normal and the only strange thing was the rain, which is pretty rare in California and more so in December. When I came back I looked for my cat but I couldn't find him. At some point I decided to go out and I ended up knocking on the door of the neighbor who lived across me. He was a forty-five year old that would give me a charming look here and there despite him being married. I would only smile back at his attempts. He had a couple of dogs and every once in a while my cat liked to pay them a visit and rile them up. That might have been why I thought my neighbor had something to do with the disappearance of my cat, I was convinced he didn't like the animal and maybe he had done something to him. When I knocked on his door he opened it and I barged in screaming incoherences and shouting my cat's name. The poor man tried to reason with me but I kept looking for my pet. I went from screaming to violence and I started breaking things up in his home.

In the middle of my attack I passed out. I can't tell how much time transpired but I must have been unconscious on the floor for several minutes. When I opened my eyes my son was in front of me, my neighbor had asked him to help him with this embarrassing situation. It was useless, the worse was yet to come.

I couldn't recognize my son. I only saw two men trying to prop me up. The first thing that came to my mind was that I had been raped. I started screaming at the top of my lungs, and I couldn't stop saying that the man in front of me was assaulting me. My son and my neighbor tried to calm me down but I was stark raving mad. I got up, pushed them and ran out the back of my neighbor's house. I jumped a fence and went into the garden of another house, and I fell flat on my face. My neighbor, frightened by this, had called the cops and my son was calling my daughter to come help him.

The only thing going through my mind was praying and asking god to not let them catch me. I felt I was walking on the edge of an abyss, about to fall straight into hell. I thought they wanted to rape me. In the midst of my prayers the police arrived, or so I'm told because I can't remember. They told me that the two agents struggled to put me under control despite my modest 115 pounds. My neighbor and the cops thought I was a drug addict and that I had to be overdosing on something. I was cuffed and put in the patrol just as my daughter Crystal arrived.

The two cops were ready to take me to the station but my daughter was able to convince them that I needed medical attention, that I didn't do drugs and that I was a bounty hunter that knew the law pretty well. I guess they saw me in such a bad shape that they decided to call an ambulance. The neighbor was so worried that he didn't want to insist on me being detained. When the firefighters and the EMT's came I felt relief, that much I can remember.

My children had called Carlos several times but he hadn't answered. They thought he didn't have the phone at hand. Much later, they told me that as soon as I was admitted to the hospital they decided to call Carlos' parents to let him know what had happened. His dad answered and told them we had split. They mentioned he was very blunt and that he warned that Carlos was not going to take any calls or go to any hospital.

This piece of news must have shocked them. The man they saw as part of the family for four years, their friend, their mom's boyfriend, had gone without saying a word. In the middle of the disappointment that bit of information helped them understand and make connections about this episode. Today, I feel embarrassed that my children had to see that scene. It mustn't be easy for kids to see their mom unconscious on a stretcher, all skin and bones, with mud on her clothes, her hair undone, and her eyes lost. That's how I looked like while I waited in the emergency room for a doctor.

A friend of Crystal's had heard about my episode and she made a diagnosis, one that had nothing to do with the study of medicine but instead with the wisdom of the soul.

"I'm sure your mom hasn't eaten in days. You have to give her something to eat."

In the ER they hadn't given me anything, not even a glass of water. My daughter bought a sandwich and I wolfed it down without objection. They told me that in that very moment I asked for Carlos, over and over. I couldn't remember what had happened with him.

"Mom, are you like this because Carlos left?" My daughter asked.

Even though she repeated the question several times I wasn't listening. I just wanted her to call him.

"Call Carlos. I want him to come here" I insisted.

After waiting for a long time in the ER I was evaluated by a doctor. It was a quick consult because he didn't find a problem with my body, so he sent me to a psychiatric hospital where I remained in observation.

We had to wait for a few hours for my transfer and during that time I didn't want to talk to anybody. I wanted to be by myself. Besides that sandwich I don't remember eating anything else. When I was transferred to the psychiatric hospital I was evaluated once more by a doctor.

"Do you know why you're here?" He asked.

I didn't know what to answer. After a while he asked me another question, one that to this day still echoes in my head.

"Do you want to end your life?"

I never thought that someone could ask me that, I always had this image of myself as being a woman that only wanted the best for herself. No matter how difficult the situation I always had a smile on my face, a good attitude, and aways loving being alive.

"No, I don't want to kill myself!" I answered without a doubt.

The doctor explained to me that I had to remain in observation for twelve hours so that they could see how my emotional state evolved. Even though he didn't give a diagnosis he warned me I could be suffering from bipolar disorder or schizophrenia.

The hospital where they took me belongs to Riverside County. There I found people with major mental problems. I was shocked to see a man, six feet tall, being strapped to a gurney from top to bottom. Another patient had an absent look, as if he wasn't in this world.

I decided to sit in a corner, alone and away from everyone and everything. I was cold. I tried to cover myself with a blanket and I closed my eyes, trying to go back to a time where I was happy with my children, my mother, and my boyfriend. The only thing I wanted now was to go back home.

After the mandatory twelve hours they called my daughter to come pick me up. I don't remember being given any medicine, although I have no memory of eating anything that day. Clearly, it was all forgotten. Though I don't think anybody would like to remember being in such a grim place.

Crystal took me home. She still didn't know how to deal with me, she was anxious because she knew her mother wasn't well. In the middle of her despair she decided to call Gabby one of my oldest friends. Even though she lived in Texas at the time, she was visiting California and came by.

She arrived the day before Christmas.

"What the hell happened Nora? Are you out of your mind?" She asked while trying to find the friend that she had known for more than two decades.

My look and my attitude alerted Gabby and after being with me for a couple of minutes she called her sister, a psychologist, to ask for help. Once she knew the reason behind my depressive state her sister instructed her to take away my phone, my car keys, my money and ID. She made it very clear that I needed to sleep. I started asking for Carlos once more as if I was back in time and didn't remember anything at all.

My friend tried to reason with me and make me understand, she wanted to help me, she never meant to harm me. With my daughter's approval Gabby gave me a combination of Benadryl and melatonin to help me sleep but it did the opposite. Minutes after taking those pills I was hysterical, I lost control, I cried and screamed at the same time. In the middle of all this I begged to be taken to the hospital. All this happened in front of my two kids, my granddaughter and my friend.

Gabby thought that the best option was to handle this new breakdown at home. She took advantage of me calming down (probably out of exhaustion from all the crying and screaming) and she took me to my bed. I laid down and started crying. She sat by my side and consoled me, I fell asleep on her lap like a child who's just had a tantrum and needs her mom to pamper her. I would wake up, scared, not knowing where I was, but I would go back to sleep thanks to the embrace of my friend. Her comforting words assured me that this would pass and that everything was going to be alright.

Sunrise came once more. It was December 24th, Christmas Eve. From a young age my children were accustomed to celebrate the birth of Jesus, and our home was always the focal point for family and friends. There was always food on our table and I made sure my home was always spotless. On that date the gifts would appear magically under the tree, but that 24th was different. That Christmas Eve marked the only day we didn't celebrate anything in my home.

My friend proposed to visit our old neighborhood in Inglewood, where her family still lives and which is very close to my father's house. Without thinking it twice I said yes and started packing, leaving my children behind. There was something inside me that wanted me to get away, I guess I just wanted to run away from all my memories (or lack thereof).

The trip to Inglewood from Menifee is almost a two hour drive. We arrived at Gabby's parents around noon and that same afternoon we went to visit my dad. It was strange for him to see me around those dates in his place, without my kids and my boyfriend. He knew Carlos wouldn't leave me alone. I don't think he noticed my emotional state, or maybe he did, I never asked him.

Though one of my sisters had one thing to say upon hearing about my brief visit to the psychiatric unit:

"Just send her to the nuthouse!"

She had grown apart from the family since the death of our mother and she didn't want to contact us after that. I think she blamed us for my mom's passing. Even though her kids work with me, my contact with her was almost null. With this in mind, I wasn't surprised by her reaction. I said goodbye to my dad and went back to Gabby's house. I looked like a child waiting while the grown ups were visiting family, never out of sight, always under surveillance. I must have been the kind of kid that looked on the verge of another tantrum. But this was natural, after all my friend had taken my cellphone, my purse, and my car, so I felt kidnapped.

Christmas came and like the song said "Christmas is here and I'm not with you". You didn't need to be a fortune teller to know I was about to have another crisis. I started crying and asked to go home. Gabby spoke on the phone with a mutual friend, but she didn't know I was listening.

"She's not looking good, I don't know what to do with her." She said, anguished.

They were so concerned that they decided to talk to a neighbor who had gone through a severe bout of depression. The man recommended I pay a visit to his therapist. In the morning of the 26th of December Gabby took me back home and gave the information to my daughter so that she could book an appointment. To make things worse, Crystal was running out of money, I was the one who handled all the accounts and all the money in the house. At the time, I was spending almost $10,000 a month. Between food, the mortgage, the bills, and the insurance on the bail bond company the grand total approached the five digits. Without cash, Crystal had to borrow $350 for my appointment with the psychologist. I arrived to that appointment without being very conscious of what was happening around me.

"What do you make of the situation with Carlos?" That was her first question.

I was speechless.

"Do you know he left you?" She insisted, as if wanting to twist the dagger I had in my heart.

"Why do you want to see Carlos if he wasn't with you in a moment like this?"

But I didn't want to understand. I just repeated that he was going to come back.

The therapists' diagnosis was more comforting than the one I had received at the hospital. I had a brief reactive psychosis. This ailment consists of a sudden display of psychotic behavior, like hallucinations or delirium, that occur because of a stressful event. To me, the most important part of this diagnosis is that people may or may not be conscious of their behavior during one of these episodes. It helped justify my erratic behavior and my denial to accept Carlos had left me. Not eating or sleeping made things worse. But I understood this, much, much later.

When the session was over the therapist prescribed pills to make me relax, and ordered me to come back in a week. Crystal was honest with her and said she didn't have any money to pay for that medicine. My love for Carlos was dragging me through the most decadent episode in my life, and this was upsetting my loved ones. The therapist had to give me free samples of her prescription.

Back at home, Crystal tried to convince me to take them but I din't want to do it.

"I'm not crazy Crystal. I'm not going to take these pills." I said angrily.

My daughter kept insisting until she had me swallow them with a sip of water. I can't say I felt the effects immediately. The only thing that I felt was the sudden realization that the year was about to end and I hadn't prepared anything. I went back to my kitchen and made a ham and cheese sandwich. I remember enjoying it, it made me want to eat again. I decided to make some enchiladas to bid the year farewell, it's one of the recipes I cook best.

Everything seemed to go back to normal. A friend from San Diego came by with her boyfriend to say hello. I was chatting with them normally until she brought Carlos into the conversation.

Just hearing his name would make my head spin, as if a part of my brain was unplugged and I couldn't understand the reality I was living in. I began asking for my ex-boyfriend again.

And yes!, you guessed it, everyone was getting sick with my attitude. Fifteen days had gone by since he had left and I didn't want to accept it. The situation was so unbearable for my family that my son even screamed in my face:

"Carlos is dead mom. Dead! Understand that."

In my state, however, I made sense of it by thinking he had actually passed away and dying was the reason behind his absence.

"So that's what happened. Carlos died! And you didn't want to tell me." I said.

Even though this was the first time my friend was dealing with this sort of problem she was the one responsible for making me understand how pathetic this show was.

"Your son is telling you that to make you understand he left. Carlos left you!"

I had hear that phrase constantly but my friend's words felt like a slap across the face. As if I understood the show I was making by not admitting he had left. My friend left and I greeted 2014 by binging movies, very much like I did when my mom passed away.

At least my mind began to understand that my relationship with Carlos was over. With that being said, I felt something was missing, I felt I needed an explanation as to why Carlos had decided to leave. Maybe he had given me a reason, or maybe that answer was buried deep inside of me, but I needed to hear that from him.

In the middle of my depression and my anxiety a voice inside of me urged me to exercise. Subconsciously, I heeded that inner call and I would wake up early every day to get into my gym clothes. But that was it. I couldn't do anything else, I couldn't get out of the house. I would sit on the couch watching television. The days went by like this until my daughter decided to leave with my grand-daughter.

"Mom, I need some space" She said, trying to soften the blow.

"I have a daughter and I can't let her see you defeated and in this condition." She added.

It wasn't the first time my daughter moved out of my house. When my mother passed away she left looking for greener pastures.

Without my grand-daughter around I had even more time to watch movies, but this was only possible as long as there was electricity at my house. My business had been paralyzed for several weeks, nobody was working and the bills were piling up on top of my kitchen table. One of my most important tools was the phone, it's where people call to ask for our services. If nobody answers the phone, however, the clients are not going to come knock on my door.

My problem with the phone was that every time I had it in my hands I wanted to cry or call Carlos. Now I understand the desire of dialing a number hoping to hear the voice of a person on the other side of the line, or at least their breathing. I wanted to steal that breath away from Carlos and see if that was enough to kickstart my existence once more. I was left with nothing but my hopes, Carlos had changed his phone number and had taken down his social media accounts.

His parents had also asked my children to stop calling because he was in a bad shape (Ha!). As a mother I understood them wanting to support their son and I made my children respect that decision. All of that didn't take away the urge to call him until something stopped me from doing so. The power company shut the power off of my house. For the first time in fifteen years since I had bought that home I was behind in my bills and my mortgage.

My love sickness was about to make me lose one of the things I had fought the most in my life. My house is the symbol of my hard work, of my tenacity, of what a single mother of two that didn't finish high school can do. Besides, it's a gorgeous house, it has five rooms, a huge living room, a big kitchen and it's tastefully decorated. The patio is full of plants and flowers and next to the pool, it's my paradise. Living without power in the house illustrated my reality. The light that always characterized me was fading. And there was only one way out of this, calling back all the clients that wanted to get out of prison, so that I could get out of mine. Ironic, I know. The problem was that I couldn't charge my cellphone.

Several days went by and I did nothing. I thought that by having the phone on my hand and answering a call or two I was on the road to recovery. At least I was conscious that my ex boyfriend hadn't passed away, he had left me. That was a big step for me.

We had a good relationship with Carlos, we were a couple that talked about everything, always trying to solve our problems. Now that I think about it, in the four years we were together we didn't have that many discussions. We were understanding of each other, we were always aware of one another. When one of us had a problem or was going through a rough patch the other was unconditionally supportive. He saved me from being raped, he was my knight in shining armor rescuing his princess. Months after the incident he had been by my side during the passing of my mother. He even loved me when I was fatter and fifteen years older than him.

"So, what happened?" I asked myself everyday.

The "why's" had become a constant in my mind. Why did he decide to leave? Why didn't he let me talk at that time? Why didn't he want to hear my side of things? Why did he stop loving me? Why, why, why? Because my mind could not find the answers to any of the questions that weighed on me I decided to get them from him. I went to look for him. But, I didn't go to ask him to take me back. I just wanted an explanation.

He had moved back with his parents. His family had a really nice house, it was almost a mansion. I drove there, a bit anguished, because I didn't know what I was going to find. From afar I could see that he was standing in the balcony that faced the entrance, he spotted my car immediately. The closer I got to the parking spot the more nervous I was. I couldn't even get out of the car when I heard his voice when my confidence tanked.

"Go away, I don't want to see you." He said.

"Carlos the only thing I want is to talk to you, we need to talk." I answered.

It was obvious he really didn't want to talk to me but I kept insisting.

"Carlos, just give me a minute." I begged.

He interrupted me in a manner never seen in the four years of our relationship.

"No! Go away, I told you I don't want to see you anymore."

Without saying another word he turned around and got inside. He left me there, alone, and without answers. Of course, I didn't understand at the time that other people don't have those answers. I don't think Carlos could explain or even answer my questions. I had those answers all along, deep inside me. He was protecting himself at his parents' home, like a scared child that doesn't want to face the problem. And what else could I hope for?

By then, Carlos was twenty six, while the woman that was trying to get him to talk was forty-two.

Age was no longer a barrier between us, it was what we wanted in life. He wanted to have kids and I didn't want to, nor could I, fifteen years ago I had surgery to prevent this. Maybe Carlos wanted to work hard to have his own business and a house he could pick on his own. None of these justifications went through my mind as I saw him disappear inside his house. The only thing I could think of was that I had hit rock bottom. I felt alone, and without anything else going on in my life I decided to go back home.

10.

NOT ALL WAS LOST

A T THAT TIME Nora Veronica didn't exist, it was as if I had vanished. Most of my friends stopped calling and visiting me. It was logical, I no longer went out for drinks I and wasn't the queen of the party. The truth was there were no more parties. For my siblings it was as if I didn't exist and my children minded their own business. The only one who was there was my dad, but as a widower, it wasn't fair to go confide him my love problems. In the midst of loneliness I began to accept that I had hit rock bottom, that I had fallen so low that the only option I had was to start climbing. Like when you jump on the deep end of the pool and you get to touch the floor. Deep down in the water there are only two possibilities, you can stay there and drown, or you kick your legs up and try to reach the surface. And that's what I did, I started to kick my legs. I paid my power bill, and I tried to take care of my finances. It wasn't that easy, but life finds a way to help you.

Trying to get out of my self-imposed lockdown and dressed in workout clothes, I made my first visit to the gym. I was skinny, very skinny. But now, it was the lack of food and water that was leaving me skeletal. After the gym, I decided to pay a visit to the coach who introduced me to bodybuilding. As soon as she saw me she made me put on my bikini. She was amazed at how thin my body was, but she didn't know what I had been through. The first thing that occurred to her was to persuade me to participate in a contest. Her enthusiasm was logical, for every contestant who enrolled there was a commission for her. That someone was making a profit off of me was the least of my worries. It was actually positive that something good would come out of this painful episode.

I said yes, I wanted to participate. But my enthusiasm wasn't the same, all I wanted was to keep myself busy. I started working out; I started a new diet, although I didn't really need it, the truth is I wasn't even hungry. Everything felt like I was starting over, but now I had a lot of experience. For example, in my business I had to go out in the morning to post bail, I kept on doing it but now I did it alone. When I was with Carlos he either accompanied me or did the procedure himself. Now, I had to do everything solo.

My workout routine for this contest didn't change; But I decided to do it by myself, without the coach's help. I started by solidifying certain muscles. My muscle memory, the knowledge stored in my body, kicked in to show me the way forward and to remind me what I had accomplished before.

"I have to take my life back, I have to do it" I said this to myself every time I could.

Finally the day of the competition arrived. It was a small contest. I was so skinny it looked like I had worked out for longer than I actually did. At the event I met one of the main nutrition promoters, a charming man named Bruce. After talking several minutes he said his brand could sponsor me.

"I'm an amateur, sponsorships are for pros." I answered him

"Then you're going to be the first amateur my company sponsors"

Bruce had one demand: I had to compete regularly. Sponsorship included sing up fees for future competitions and nutrition products. The idea excited me, it was a new challenge, something that I could do on my own without depending on anybody to accomplish this. I even entertained the idea of turning professional. I told my trainer about the offer and the idea of moving up to professional competitions. She immediately warned me not to get my hopes up, I was forty-two and at that age it would be hard to jump to the highest echelons in bodybuilding.

Her words didn't make a dent on my confidence. I started working out, sculpting my body. But this time I was very conscious that I wanted to open a path for myself in the world of muscle.

Around those days, and almost by destiny, I heard back from Gustavo Vargas a television reporter that I had met some years back. Gustavo worked in sports and without thinking twice I told him about my new adventure. As I had anticipated my story got his attention and he started shooting a story about bodybuilding. When my trainer saw the television cameras come in she was fascinated, she was a businesswoman first, and she knew that this opportunity would help her promote her business. This reminded me of my youth and the world of promotional modeling, when I displayed my many charms to talk to people. I enjoyed watching myself in television, and physically I was on the path to recovery. You couldn't tell I was heartbroken and those images motivated me even more to workout. I focused on taking care of my nutrition, I always ate healthy and made sure to drink a lot of water.

Not long after, in the middle of one of my workouts I met with my son. I told him all about my new adventure and I told him how excited I was at the idea of becoming a pro. He looked me square in the eyes and said:

"Mom, how can you make sure that everything that happened is not going to happen again?"

He was talking about those days full of delirium, crying, and hysteria, when I didn't even wanted to know what was happening. My son was right to ask me that question in the manner that he did, coldly, succinctly, without reservations. It felt like another slap in the face for me. All of a sudden I saw what my life had been for the past month as if I was watching a movie. A series of questions then came to my mind: Are you stupid Nora? Were you madly in love? Can't you live without Carlos? I realized that the answer to those questions was no. Truthfully, since the moment I left my parent's house I never needed a man to survive, I was always the provider, I was always taking care of everyone.

So, what happened to me?

My son interrupted my inner monologue and told me seriously:

"I need you to make sure that this is not going to happen again."

With that demand he turned around and left. This ultimatum, from my seventeen year-old child, stuck in my mind. Every time I did aerobic exercises, like running or walking, I started to think about this. Even when I was lifting weights I would start a conversation with myself, these dialogues did a lot of good to my body and soul. Thinking about this for so long made me realize that I saw Carlos as my savior. He saved me from a rape attempt and stopped my assailant and for this I put him on a pedestal.

That was a problem I had not only with my ex boyfriend but with other people too. I valued too much what others did for me and I didn't appreciate my own contributions. There was still a bit of that insecurity that was born after I left school, because I thought I wasn't very smart, and maybe because I am a woman too. I wasn't the kind of woman that took credit for what I did. However, I was slowly beginning to appreciate my efforts.

Soon after, my chance to win professional qualification came. I was no longer skinny, my body looked thin but with strong muscles and you could see that lifting weights was getting me some results. I was surprised at winning first place. I won with a score that allowed me to enter the professional circuit. My next goal was to be a part of the United States team.

Professionals in bodybuilding receive money awards when they participate in tournaments. Generally, sponsors pay entry fees among other things. So taking this step helped me with my economic situation because I no longer had to spend money. On the contrary, now I would be able to profit from bodybuilding. This motivated me even more to give myself to this sport. There was also the fact that I was doing something for myself. Nobody is helping you lift those weights or run that extra mile, so whenever I would look myself in the mirror I would see the results of my own effort.

On the days that followed I focused on winning my category. I was going to compete in the bikini classification, the same category that won me my first trophy ever. As the name indicates you have to parade in a two-piece swimsuit while the jury evaluates the harmony of your body. You have to be thin, or as they say: "Well-done". The muscles must be defined but the contestant can't lose her femininity. They also judge symmetry, meaning how proportionate the body of the contestant is. I am 5'2" and I weighed 115 pounds. To dazzle them with my body I would have to focus on my buttocks because I didn't have that much.

I had taken care of my breasts a few years back with implants, and with exercise the had recovered their strength. Now the challenge was to balance my glutes with my chest. For this I had to strengthen my legs, and the muscles in my abdomen had to be even stronger. Even though I had been practicing bodybuilding for more than two years I wasn't sure that I could get my buttocks to grow.

It sounds sarcastic but I tried to get Carlos out of my mind by focusing on my ass. Thankfully I was able to do both, The first one was simpler, the second one was a little bit harder to achieve. I was able to forget Carlos because of the conversations I had with myself. It's as if I had changed him for me. I fell in love with Nora and I understood that a relationship with another person wasn't going to work if I didn't love myself first. It sounds a bit cheesy but that's what happened to me. The part about my buttocks was true as well. It was harder because it needed determination, physical strength, and enduring a bit of pain.

One of the best exercises to make your glutes grow are squats, specially those that involve carrying a certain weight over your shoulders. I started carrying 10 pounds, and then I added five pounds until I was able to put 185 pounds on my shoulders. That was literally harder than forgetting my ex-boyfriend, when I squatted 185 the weight of his departure didn't feel that heavy in my life.

By that time I was eating plenty of meat. In bodybuilding there's the belief that animal protein is more effective than vegetable protein for the development of muscle. My diet was based in consuming very little carbohydrates, a lot of water, vitamins, some vegetables and meat, poultry and fish, the latter being one of my favorites. The diet given by my trainer was now a thing of the past. I started getting interested in food, its nutrients, and how I could spice up my menu.

I learned that proteins are essential for life and are responsible, in grand part, for almost every vital process like organ function, growth, tissue repair, among others. The quantity of daily protein in a diet depends on a person's age, weight and physical activity. The National Academy of Medicine created a system called the Dietary Reference Intake (DRI) that provides guidelines about what we should eat on a healthy diet. According to the DRI a person should eat 0.8 grams of protein for every kilogram of weight per day. I did the math for 118 pounds which was my weight at that time, I applied the formula [118 x

2.2 x 0.8] and found out I had to consume about 42.4 grams of protein a day. Doctors say that this is the adequate amount for a person with average weight that doesn't exercise a lot. However I was an athlete using great amounts of energy, and on top of that I wanted to build muscle.

Coaches in bodybuilding recommend consuming 1.5 of the competitor's weight in grams of protein. Following those recommendations, I was ingesting almost 200 grams of proteins per day. I followed all the indications of my colleagues with discipline. I cooked at home and I froze the portions that I had to eat throughout the week, all measured to a "T". I also didn't give up to the temptation of the cravings everyone has when we're dieting. My daily exercise routine and diet were more becoming something I could handle. If astronauts and soldiers can withstand restrictions in their diet, why couldn't I do it?

The victories came soon after and I won the points needed to be part of the United States team. My life was on a good track once more, the shape of my body and the joy that had returned were opening new doors and giving me new adventures. I was even hired to be the image of several products, I was back to promotional modeling, but this time I was modeling at forty-four years old

11.

NIGHTMARE IN THE EMERGENCY ROOM

O N SEPTEMBER 2015, two weeks before one of the most important competitions in the world of bodybuilding I had one of those busy days. I woke up early to sort some clothes for a photoshoot and I had my breakfast and my vitamins. Before going to the photographer's studio I went to the gym to workout. At the gym I started feeling as if the world started spinning around me, akin to what I felt when I was choosing my mother's coffin. As I did in that occasion I decided to go to the bathroom. I barely made it in when I threw up. A woman who was there approached me and asked me how I felt. I was on the ground and about to pass out. I tried to muster some strength to get up but the weakness and the dizziness didn't let me. I knew I couldn't get out of that situation by myself, I needed help. I asked the woman to look for a friend that I had seen on my way in. The lady went out in a hurry as I was trying to catch my breath. My friend Eric arrived and helped me get on my feet. I asked him to take me home, I needed to lie down for a while.

On the road my nausea came back. My head kept spinning. Eric was very worried, he insisted on asking me where he should take me. He saw me in such a state that he said the ER was the best place for me to go. I insisted that I wanted to go home. When we arrived, he helped me get out of the car, but I couldn't find the keys of the house. As soon as I went in I had to go to the bathroom immediately, I wanted to vomit but I didn't have anything left in my stomach. I felt I had something stuck in my throat, and nothing would come out of my mouth. The nausea wasn't going away, I was weak and I barely could help myself by sitting. Since I saw nobody at home I told my friend to take me to the hospital.

I don't have very fond memories of that emergency room. The last time I was there I was suffering a mental breakdown because Carlos had left me. It had been a year-and-a-half so the first thing the doctor wanted to know was how I felt emotionally. I told him, I was stable, that the reason for my visit was my nausea. My condition between December of 2013 and then was very different. I had gained weight, my muscles were bulging, and apart from looking a bit pale my skin looked wonderful. The only problem was pain.

Not being very convinced of my emotional recovery, the doctor asked if I had taken anything. But there wasn't anything different beyond my natural diet and the vitamins and supplements I was taking. He ordered some routine exams that showed nothing to worry about. The only thing he could say was that he saw I was dehydrated, and his diagnosis was spot on. I had been on a competition two weeks before and to increase my chances of winning I stopped my ingest of water as I had done in the past. This is common practice among bodybuilders, to reduce fluid consumption before going to the stage with the objective of dropping weight. A dried up muscle will be easier for the judges to notice. That's the final touch in the fine art of bodybuilding.

The planned dehydration starts almost a week before the competition, with some athletes consuming distilled water to help in the process. Consumption of liquids keeps decreasing until you can't drink anything at all. On day zero you're barely wetting your lips. Because I knew I was dehydrated he couldn't say anything of use. he prescribed some pain medication, I think it was morphine. He also prescribed other pills to help me digest food. I knew that this wasn't the problem but I didn't refute him. He's the doctor and patients don't seem to have the right to say something. But even though we didn't go to med school sometimes we know our body better. I was discharged twelve hours later.

The pain medicine worked and as soon as I started to feel better I decided to stop taking the pills. I started training shortly after. Two weeks after my visit to the hospital I was parading my body in a bikini at a bodybuilding competition. I had dehydrated my body again. I wasn't going to fail in my goal to be part of the United States team. I won in every category I competed in. But even though I came back home with several medals I also came back with a pain in my stomach that barely let me breathe.

The same scene of two weeks ago was repeating itself, only that this time the symptoms were worse. The route to the hospital was the same. I was on the emergency room with a body that on the outside looked spectacular but didn't look that good on the inside. A doctor read my file in detail and asked me if I practiced any sports. In the middle of the wretched state I found myself in I was able to tell him how I prepared myself to win every trophy I had gotten until that day. The diagnosis was far more accurate this time, the doctor had finally found out what was happening to me. My liver was about to collapse because of the amount of animal protein I was eating.

The problem with beef, or pork, is that the digestive system needs more time to process it in comparison with vegetables. Poultry and fish are also harder to digest and spend more time in our bodies if you compare them to a carrot or a leaf of lettuce.

You have to remember that I was eating almost 200 grams of protein a day. This was terrible.

My liver was so stressed it almost reached breaking point. To make things worse I deprived my liver of the water it needed to function. I was literally killing myself. I was lucky that I hadn't suffered kidney failure too. The liver and kidneys work in tandem so if one of them sings out of tune the other one will start losing its rhythm. With this diagnosis at hand the doctor told me that I had to stop my diet. Hearing this was devastating, I was a few weeks away from a competition to qualify for a spot in the national team, to have the chance to represent the United States, to wear the flag of the country I was born in. I was conscious that I wasn't going to the Olympics where the best athletes of the world go, but this competition was where the best in bodybuilding competed. I had gotten there after many failures, and at a much older age than the athletes that begin practicing this sport.

I came back home trying to find an answer to this problem. I couldn't keep playing with my health. Of all the things that had happened in my life this visit to the hospital scared me the most. I thought I wasn't going to make it out alive. I knew I was killing myself, but on the other hand, I didn't want to bury my dreams of going to the bodybuilding Olympics. My biggest problem was consuming so much animal protein. Until that moment I had never thought I could replace them with another food item with the same properties, one that my body could digest better. Coincidentally, my daughter had been a vegetarian for more than a year and even had my granddaughter in that same regimen. When she heard about my situation, Crystal gave me all the information about how a vegetarian diet works.

I tried to recover in the weeks that followed. I reduced my consumption of red meat and I tried to replace it with fish. The days went by quickly and in the blink of an eye I was competing again. My condition wasn't the best but I made it to the fourth place in my category among all the contestants in the country. The most important thing was that I achieved my dream to be in the United States team that would go compete in Europe next year.

As soon as I got home I invited my granddaughter to eat. I felt like breaking my diet and I was craving for some pancakes with bacon. They were my favorite guilty pleasure. I was about to order them when my granddaughter took my hand and tenderly said:

"In heaven they don't eat little piggies. My grandmother Abelina said they don't eat piggies in heaven."

I was surprised with what she told me. But I remembered that my granddaughter used to mention speaking with my mom. The one she always called "Abuelita". She would see her in the yellow butterflies that were always in our garden. To be honest, we didn't pay much attention to what she said because we thought those are things children say. Something changed that day, I felt that what she had heard was true and that it was a message from above. I decided to cancel the order and I was left thinking about all of this. I didn't want to stop practicing the sport that made me feel so good with myself. By then I had won twenty-one trophies and nineteen first places. But I knew that if I wanted to continue I had to do something different. So I made a New Year's resolution: I would become a vegetarian in 2016. I stopped eating red meat, chicken and fish. I only stuck with eggs, especially the whites because they are healthy. I also kept consuming dairy, milk, yogurt and cheese. The challenge was to maintain my muscle mass without eating animal protein. Very few professional bodybuilders had tried to be vegetarians, few kept competing, and hardly any had won.

As you know, I'm laser focused when I have something in my mind. Broccoli became one of my biggest allies, ninety-six grams of this vegetable is the equivalent to 3 grams of animal protein. You can make the math in your head on the amount of broccoli I had to eat to replace all the red meat protein. I learned how to cook it in different ways so I wouldn't get bored to eat it. I was doing this consciously, I wanted my body to be well inside and out. I had understood that the body was like a musical instrument, the more you tune it, the better it sounds.

Qualifiers for the United States Natural Bodybuilding Team, 2015

Winning this competition allowed me to participate in the World Championship in Budapest, Hun-gary in 2016.

Personal album, 2015

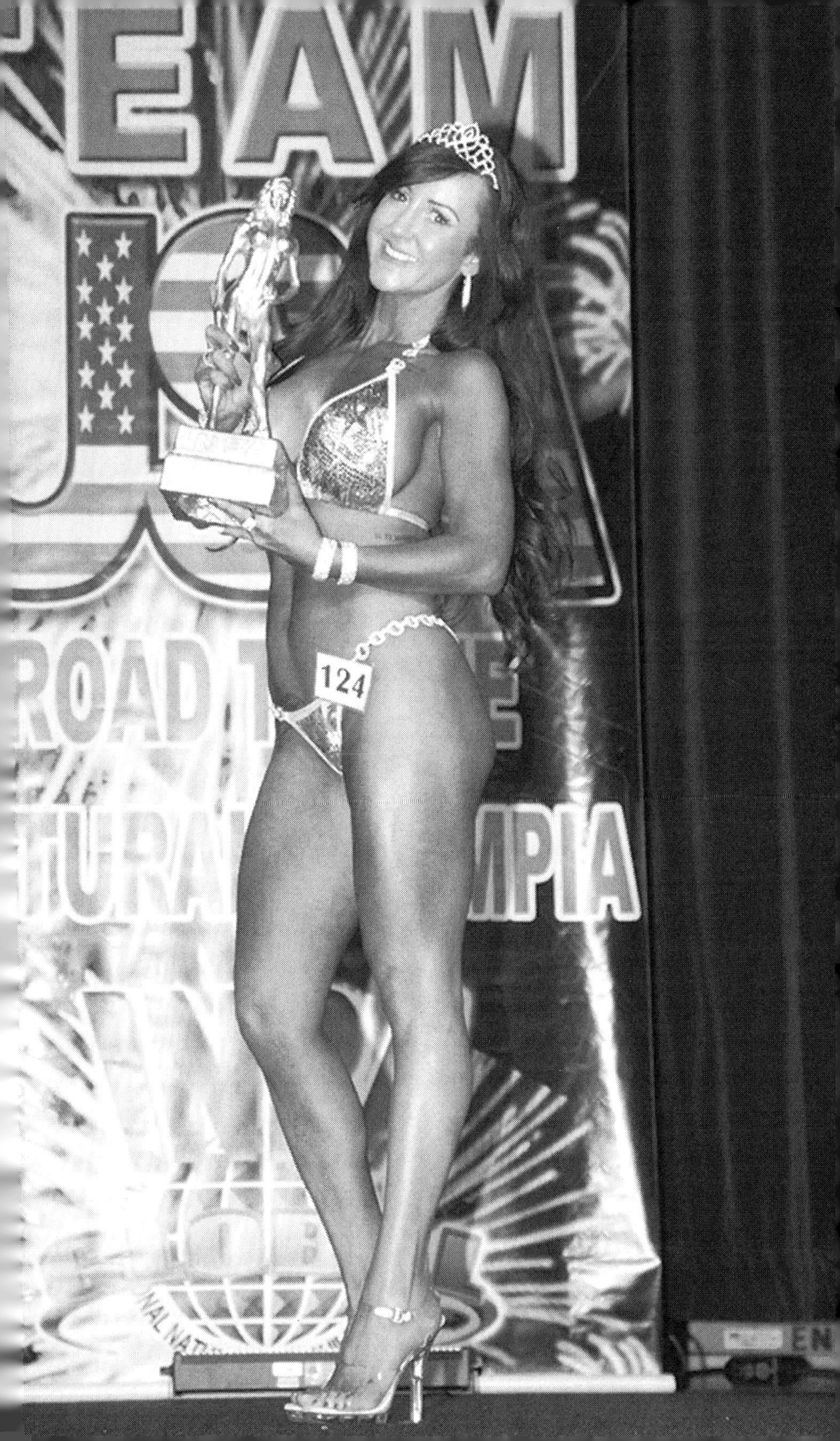
124

12.

BUDA... WHAT?

MY BODY AND SPIRIT were in harmony. Now only the trip to the Bodybuilding Olympics remained. Budapest, capital of Hungary was the final destination. When I hear that word I thought deep inside:

"Buda... What? Where the hell is that city?

Remember, I'm unschooled and Budapest didn't ring a bell. I didn't even know where it was. They explained to me that it was in Europe and for me that seemed enough, I had always dreamed of exploring that continent. Since I was with Carlos I dreamt that someday we would spend some of our lives over there. We dreamt with visiting Venice, one of the most romantic cities in the world. Venice and Paris, in my opinion, should be in every couple's bucket list. But now I was going to travel by myself. This didn't make me sad, just a bit anxious.

The United States team was made of twelve athletes. Other members of the group travelled to participate as amateurs. My plane ticket and expenses had been taken care of by my sponsor. Without having to worry about money, the only thing I had to worry about was winning. I left the minutiae of my travel to one of my teammates, she had participated a year back in Dubai and she knew how to do everything. She was even taking her mom to the competition. I gave her all my money and she arranged everything for me.

Then came the day of the trip. I learned that for these competitions you have to take your own food. I'm not kidding. Athletes can't know if the hotel they're staying in will have all the food required by their strict diet. Therefore, most bodybuilders carry with them all the meals they will consume throughout the tournament. I was carrying two bags, one of them had my vitamins, my meals, and a good number of boiled eggs. We had decided to meet with my friend at Los Angeles International Airport, I was restless and excited so I went out early with my two bags and my boiled eggs for my two hour trip to the airport. At the airport she handed me my ticket.

The time to board the plane had come, it was going to be the beginning of my new adventure, but when I went through immigration the officer looked at me and said:

"You can't travel with this passport."

"Why?" I asked.

"It expired."

I couldn't believe it. I had brought my old passport. I had renewed it months before but in my hurry to leave the house I had brought the old one. The plane would leave in two hours, the exact amount of time it would take to get back home. I wouldn't be able to make it. Our plan was to travel on a Tuesday, arrive on Wednesday, rest on Thursday and enter the competition on Friday. This meant I still had a day to spare. Without being able to do anything else, I said goodbye to my friend and saw her leave for Hungary.

The airline changed my ticket and I would travel the following day. This time, with my new passport in hand and a bag full of hopes and hard boiled eggs, I travelled alone and without a lot of information. My friend had planned the whole itinerary and I hadn't even bothered to learn anything about my new destination. I only had the hotel's address, I didn't even know what language was spoken in Budapest. I also didn't know you were supposed to exchange Dollars to Euros.

I arrived in Budapest one day before the competition. I felt like Cinderella looking at the castle for the first time. And this is not a metaphor, the town was full of old castles right by the Danube River. I think most fairy tales must have been inspired by this beautiful city. But the best part of all this? I was there.

Nora Veronica Reynoso, Abelina's daughter, the bounty hunter, the vegetarian bodybuilder that was about to accomplish one of her goals: To win. The medal would become the symbol of victory after so many lost battles.

However, there were another five hundred competitors from all over the world with the same dream and determination to win. When the day of the competition arrived every contestant showed their immaculate presentation and their excellent condition. I observed them and wondered: What are you showing differently? I didn't even get to answer that because my name was announced and I had to go on stage. When I started my demonstration I realized that each step I took, each movement I made, every single one of my muscles was the product of an incessant search for harmony and wellness in my being. And I did it.

I won.

I took the gold medal in my category. But this wasn't just about the medal hanging on my neck, the applause, or the prize. This was about the feeling of triumph, and the glory of healing my mind, body and spirit. The best part of this fairy tale is that the spell didn't break at midnight. The princess didn't run, the chariot didn't vanish. On the contrary, after that day, other dreams came true.

Gold Medal in the Bikini category. INBA/PNBA World Championships in Natural Body-building. Budapest, Hungary. 2016.

"My dreams came true, and they opened the door to a new life."

Photo by: Csakisti Photograpy, 2016.

13.

TELLING MY HISTORY

THERE IS AN OLD SAYING in my family that goes: "Nobody learns in someone else's head". It's about how you can only find the solutions to your problems through your own errors. And before I lived through this odyssey, I always thought like this. I believed that I could only learn from my own mistakes, it even seemed that, subconsciously, I wanted to destroy myself to be able to learn the lesson, and find the way of pulling myself together.

The elation of being crowned champion in Budapest allowed me to see the chain of self-destruction that had been dragging me for a while. After the competition, in the middle of my tour of Europe, I understood that human beings have many chances to be wrong in the course of their life, but they also have the chances to avoid all those mistakes in the first place. When I landed in Venice, Italy, I wondered: Why didn't I listen to Lupita sooner? Why didn't the doctor explain the importance of good nutrition to overcome a loss? I should have paid attention to all the signs that my body was sending me before collapsing. Acting in time would have spared me from so much physical and psychological pain.

Sitting in Saint Mark's Square, looking at the sea and the gondolas, I did a stroll down memory lane, reminiscing about everything that happened after my mom's passing. I came to the conclusion that most of my emotional issues originated in how insecure I felt with some aspects in my life. This insecurity made me neglect things as basic as my eating habits and even led me to drink alcohol in excess.

Walking through Venice with my friends, without any man nearby, I confirmed that to be happy with someone I had to be happy with myself first. Happiness doesn't depend on your couple, on your children, on your parents. With that lesson in my mind, I returned to California and kept on training for the following year; I wanted to prove that this medal had not been just luck. This time life took me to Rimini, a coastal village in the north of Italy, and the biggest Bodybuilding Exhibition in 2017. There were more than three thousand participants. The number of athletes in competition surpassed the five hundred in Budapest. By the end of the competition gold was hanging from my neck once more. Life was vindicating me. I was not mistaken, that the decisions I had taken in relation to my new eating habits were the right ones. I was forty-five years old and my life was enriched by new challenges.

It was precisely during this trip that I decided to tell my history. I started thinking that if I could help at least one person from committing the mistakes that took me to the hospital several times, all this would be worthwhile. I wanted to tell everyone who suffers from nutrition problems or from physical stagnation that there is a solution, and that it isn't an impossible goal to accomplish.

For many, losing weight, getting used to healthy eating habits, and doing exercise, turns into a boring and unattainable goal. We put so many obstacles to ourselves that to change our habits we even pay other people to help us make our dreams come true. Many get stuck halfway through the race, or even worse, they miss the starting gun. But I'm the example that one can reach the goal.

Now that you know my history I hope that you at least consider my recommendations, and feel motivated to take back your health and the love for yourself.

If you believe age is an issue, I have to remind you that I had turned forty-one when I started a diet and exercise regime for the first time ever; four years later I won a gold medal, and I was crowned world champion because of the muscles that I had worked so hard to develop.

For those who say that worrying for the well-being of their body is not worth it because they're too old, I give the example of Ruth Bader Ginsburg. An associate judge in the Supreme Court of the United States, who at eighty-five years old is one of the most lucid minds in our country. Bader-Ginsburg is a staunch advocate of exercise, as this is what keeps her so vital even though she is the oldest of the nine judges of the maximum court. As Justice Bader-Ginsburg, there are hundreds of thousands of seniors that stay healthy doing exercise. They discovered that this habit activates the hormones responsible for that feeling of happiness and our will to live.

In my personal research to confirm that my campaign in favor of exercise was not a whim I learned that the World Health Organization recommends at least 150 minutes of moderate exercise a week for the elderly. This is the minimum established to integrate older adults into an exercise program. In spite of these calls, most of us pay no attention until a serious health problem arises.

And if age isn't an obstacle to do exercise, diet isn't either. This idea that changing your diet is impossible is just an invisible wall which all of us stumble with; I know from experience how we rationalize things like this. Your dietary routines can be changed at any moment and at whatever age. Your eating habits are not an excuse. At age forty-four I transformed my diet completely and stopped consuming all kinds of meats. But that didn't mean I had to forget my mother's Mexican recipes, which are close to my heart; I have maintained this culinary tradition without a problem because I accommodated them to my new reality.

In the list of excuses we use before making a major change is also money. Allow me to retort, you don't need a lot of resources to take care of yourself. You don't need a personal trainer to establish an exercise routine. You can even do it at home, without going to the gym. And if we speak about a good diet, you won't need to spend a lot of money on ingredients, on the contrary, you'll save some. The only thing you need is to be conscious of is what you are putting in your mouth. "To eat with a purpose" must always be your motto.

If we have good eating habits and an exercise routine we will be prepared to face situations like heartbreak, the loss of a dear one, or more common problems. As a bounty hunter and bail agent, I witness day in and day out how a problem can knock at someone's door at any time. My advice is to be prepared mentally and physically to confront these situations.

It took a lot of time and pain for me to discover the connection that exists between happiness, your state of mind, and your body. I am not going to say that since I began exercising and eating better I have no problems anymore. I still have them, but now they are made bearable. My focus is to always find a solution.

My transformation was based on a 10-day diet that allowed me to lose 8 to 10 pounds in a short time; I have designed it to share it with you. Many of the people who experienced the results of the 10-day plan prolonged the diet up to one month in which they dropped between 14 and 18 pounds.

Another benefit of this diet is that when people begin to change their eating habits and follow all the recommendations they avoid the well-known "rebound" (putting on weight) because the body reacts better to the new eating habits and tries to maintain them. In addition to losing weight, those that have done the diet have slept better, and have reported improvement on some minor ailments. Everything is part of a process.

Along the 10-day diet I recommend a brief exercise routine that will begin to condition your body to return to physical activity.

Let's celebrate life, let's not die trying.

WARNING

The recommendations in this book, including its intermittent fasting program, diets and exercise routine are product of the private practice and research of the author and were not designed to treat or cure any disease. None of the affirmations in this book have been evaluated by the Food and Drug Administration (FDA) or in controlled clinical studies. People interested in following the recommendations laid forth in this book, specially pregnant women, people with symptoms or food disorders, endocrine patients and other health problems should consult first with a doctor.

14.

INTERMITTENT FASTING

I N MY CONSTANT SEARCH for the best trends in nutrition, and by doing them with a purpose, I found intermittent fasting. This routine consists of alternating periods of fasting with periods in which you are allowed to eat. The purpose of this is to regulate the way our organism works.

In our normal food intake, the food we ingest will end up in our cells to give us the energy required to function. If our cells don't use all that energy they will store it to use it in a different occasion. Fat is basically stored energy. Whenever we fast, however, the cells release this stored energy to sustain our body. After understanding that process I started practicing intermittent fasting and I integrated it to my daily routine with wonderful results.

There are several ways to practice intermittent fasting. I practice one of the less drastic routines called 16/8 and it consists in fasting for sixteen hours and eating during eight. At face value you might think you'll starve but it isn't like that. The first thing to consider is that you have to subtract the eight hours of sleep, on average, to those sixteen hours of fasting. So you are left with only eight hours in which you can drink all the liquid you want excluding sugary drinks.

The schedule that I recommend to practice intermittent fasting, and which applies to standard working hours, is between six in the afternoon and ten in the morning of the following day. During this period you can't ingest solid food. You can drink any kind of liquid that doesn't have sugar in it, like sodas.

If you have problems following the recommended schedule you can modify it according to your necessities. For example, if you eat breakfast at nine in the morning your last meal should be at five in the afternoon. If your first meal is at eleven in the morning the last time you can eat solid food should be seven in the evening.

Here you can find options to practice intermittent fasting. Choose one of these examples and try to stick to it for ten days during your diet.

I hope that when you discover how effective fasting can be you adopt it as part of your daily routine.

FIRST SOLID MEAL	LAST SOLID MEAL
6 AM	2 PM
7 AM	3 PM
8 AM	4 PM
9 AM	5 PM
10 AM	6 PM
11 AM	7 PM
12 AM	8 PM
1 PM	9 PM
2 PM	10 PM

15.

EATING WITH A PURPOSE

THE 10 DAY DIET

This program is designed with the 16/8 period of intermittent fasting (Sixteen hours of fasting and an eight hour block in which you can eat solid food). I recommend using the schedule that starts at 10:00 in the morning and ends at 6:00 in the afternoon. As I explained in the previous chapter, if this schedule doesn't fit your needs you can use any of the ones proposed in that list.

After consuming your first solid food you should eat every two hours for a grand total of five meals in the eight hour period.

Remember that from the moment you get up until your first meal, 10:00 AM in the example above, you can only drink liquids. The goal is to drink about a gallon of liquid a day.

Drinks you can consume:

- *Pure water, or with a lemon infusion.*
- *-Herbal tea that includes peppermint, mint, ginger, oregano, chamomile, or well known blends such as black tea or green tea.*
- *-Hibiscus tea, you can add cinnamon for extra flavor.*
- *-Coffee, I recommend adding edible cocoa butter or a spoonful of coconut oil. This will help you burn fat.*

This diet does not contain animal proteins such as beef, pork, fish, shellfish, chicken or eggs, or dairy products such as milk, butter or cheese. This diet also eliminates the ingestion of processed sugars and restricts the consumption of bread or refined flours. The consumption of alcoholic beverages is forbidden during this diet.

During the first five days of this plan you will need to drink a juice cleanse to clean your digestive system. This process will be complemented by a smoothie that will be consumed for ten days as breakfast. This will help you get rid of any waste accumulated in your intestines.

Up next, you will find a mock of what a day in this diet consists of followed by a series of recipes you can adapt to your taste, your own way of cooking, and your pocket. I advice to plan and cook your meals three days in advance. The lack of programming leads us to choose unhealthy foods like fast food. Don't let your hunger decide what you will consume. Cook the right portions and keep your food properly refrigerated. I suggest using sea salt and cayenne pepper.

Remember to always eat with a purpose.

ONE DAY GUIDELINE

Eat enough to satisfy your hunger. Remember to drink liquids before you eat and in between meals.

10: 00 am - Papaya smoothie to detoxify. (Mandatory for the first five days)

Take 2 ounces of chopped papaya with seeds, add two ounces of water and blend it. Drink cold.

10: 15 am - Kale Smoothie. (mandatory for 10 days)

- 2 large handfuls of kale, (preferably frozen)
- 1 tablespoon of almond butter
- 1/2 frozen banana
- 1 tablespoon of vegetable-based protein powder
- 1/2 cup of almond milk or water
- 4 dry dates without seed
-

Blend and drink cold. Recommendation: Put your kale in the freezer, the drink will have a better texture if you use frozen kale. This shake will helps us do a bowel cleanse because it contains large amounts of fiber.

12:00 Noon - 4 Jackfruit Tacos

- 1 cup of jackfruit pulp
- 1 chipotle chili
- 2 tomatoes
- Salt and garlic to taste
- Corn tortillas

Cook the jackfruit pulp for a few minutes in water with a pinch of salt. Add cayenne pepper if you want. For the sauce blend chipotle chile with the tomatoes, and add salt and garlic to taste.

You can add onions, cilantro and lettuce to your tacos.

Choose corn tortillas that have fewer calories.

2: 00 pm - Sautéed Tofu

- ½ cup of Tofu
- ½ cup of Pre-Cooked Beans
- ½ cup Broccoli
- Onion cut into slices
- Coconut oil

Chop the ingredients into pieces. Cook the onion until translucent. In another pan, sauté the broccoli and the beans. Mix with the onion and add the tofu, cook tofu until golden. This dish can be consumed hot or cold.

4: 00 pm - Almond yogurt.

6: 00 pm - Repeat a portion of Sautéed Tofu Jackfruit Tacos

For dessert eat 6 cherries. They are full of components that will help you sleep.

TEN RECIPES FOR A DELICIOUS DIET

Here you can find ten recipes that you can use interchangeably each day. Remember to prepare meals three days in advance. Portion your meals in cups or small dishes if you think this will help you think you are eating the right amount. If you choose to eat tacos, remember to use tortillas that have the least amount of calories possible. You can also prepare a cup of brown or parboiled rice.

Don't eat rice if you chose to eat tortillas.

You will also find three suggestions for snacks in-between meals. Pick the recipes that you like the most and always try to include plant-based protein food like garbanzo, lentils, beans, quinoa, tofu, soy or chia seeds.

1 Oatmeal for Breakfast (To eat after the kale shake or the last meal)

- ½ cup precooked oatmeal
- 2 teaspoons of chia seeds
- ½ cup of fruit (Preferably cranberries, raspberries, strawberries)
- ½ teaspoon honey or agave
- Cinnamon and vanilla extract to taste

Combine all the ingredients in a bowl, stir and let it rest for at least four hours. It's better if you prepare it the night before and keep it refrigerated. Add fresh berries before eating. This tasty snack can be eaten cold or hot.

2 Rajas Tacos with Mushrooms

- ½ cup sliced mushrooms,
- ½ cup of rajas (Roasted poblano chile strips)
- 1 Diced Tomato
- Corn tortillas
- Onion, cilantro, olive oil, cayenne pepper, and salt to taste.

Fry the mushrooms and the roasted poblano pepper strips in olive oil. Add pepper, tomato, and salt. Let it cook until desired texture is achieved.

Heat tortillas in a different pan.

Add onion, cilantro, pico de gallo sauce or avocado sauce.

You can top with vegetarian cheese.

3 Vegetable Tacos

- ½ cup chopped broccoli
- ½ cup chopped carrot
- ½ cup chopped pumpkin
- ½ cup chopped eggplant
- ½ cup chopped onion.
- Salt, cayenne pepper, and jalapeño pepper to taste.
- Olive oil.
- Corn tortillas

Sauté the onion in olive oil until translucent. Add the vegetables, salt, pepper and chilies. Let it cook until desired texture is achieved. Heat the tortillas in a different pan. Add pico de gallo sauce or avocado to your liking.

This is another recipe that could use vegetarian cheese as a topping if you wish.

4 Bean tacos with tofu

- ½ cup canned black beans
- ½ cup of crumbled tofu.
- Tomato, cumin, garlic and salt
- Olive oil
- Corn tortillas

In a pan, sauté the beans in olive oil, add cumin to taste. After a few minutes add tofu. Blend the tomatoes with garlic and salt and add this to the beans and tofu mix. Cook for five minutes.

Heat the tortillas. Add pico de gallo sauce, avocado, or vegetarian cheese.

5 Turmeric Cauliflower

- 1 cup of cauliflower.
- 1 teaspoon of paprika, black pepper and cayenne pepper.
- 1 tablespoon of turmeric powder
- 5 tablespoons of extra virgin olive oil

Preheat the oven to 350 degrees F.

Toss the chopped cauliflower with the olive oil, garlic, and red pepper on a baking sheet; Roast until golden and tender for 30 minutes.

6 Lentil salad

- 1 cup of cooked lentils
- ½ cup diced carrot
- ½ cup of chopped pumpkin
- ¼ cup of cooked corn
- You can add lettuce if you wish

For the vinaigrette use sesame oil or olive oil, 3 tablespoons of vinegar, lemon, a pinch of salt, sugar and black pepper. Add the lentils to the vinaigrette, followed by the other ingredients and stir.

7 Garbanzo with Vegetables

- 1 cup of garbanzo
- ½ cup diced carrots
- ½ cup of chopped pumpkin
- Salt, bay leaf, onion, garlic, tomato, chile serrano, and cayenne pepper,
- Coconut or olive oil

Cook the chickpeas with laurel and a bit of salt. Cook the carrot aside. Fry the onion until it is translucent, then add the garlic, tomato, chili and pumpkins. Let it cook until desired texture is achieved. Add garbanzo, carrots, and cayenne pepper to taste. Fry for a few minutes.

8 Wraps of lettuce

- 1 cup cooked and mashed garbanzo
- 1/4 cup Chopped onion
- 1/4 cup chopped celery.
- Mustard and vegan mayonnaise
- Salt, pepper and turmeric powder to taste.
- Apples, grapes or raisins (optional)
- Romaine lettuce leafs

Mix all the ingredients in a bowl and stir.
Put 3 spoons of the mix to a lettuce leaf and wrap.

9 Vegetables and Spice Soup

- ½ cup of turmeric root in pieces
- ¼ cup celery peeled and cut into small pieces
- 1 cup chopped and peeled carrots
- ½ cup of corn
- 3 peeled and chopped potatoes
- Ginger peeled and chopped into pieces to taste.
- Red peppers cut into slices to taste.
- Onion, oregano, garlic, pepper and salt to taste.

Add spices such as ginger and turmeric, and garlic to a pot with water, let it boil. Add chopped vegetables, salt and pepper to taste. If you want you can add noodles.

This soup is excellent in cold season, and it makes for wonderful comfort food when you have the flu. Most of its ingredients help fight the common cold.

10 Broccoli Soup

- 2 cups of broccoli
- ½ onion in large pieces
- 2 medium potatoes cut into pieces
- Olive oil
- Salt, garlic and pepper to taste
-

Add broccoli in a pan of boiling water and cook for 10 minutes. Add potatoes in a separate pan of boiling water and cook for 15 minutes Sauté the onion in olive oil until translucent, add chopped garlic. In a blender add broccoli, potato and the onion and garlic mix. Add salt and pepper to taste.

11 Avocado Sauce for Tacos

- Avocado Sauce for Tacos.
- ½ ripe avocado
- ¾ cup of coriander
- Lemon juice
- Salt, Pepper, Garlic.
- Olive oil

Blend all the ingredients, and add water if necessary to make the sauce less dense.

SNACK

The snack is the fourth meal of the day, taking place after lunch and before dinner.

1. Jícama chopped and peeled. Add lemon and chili to taste.
2. Cucumber slices. Add salt, lemon and chili to taste.
3. Baked eggplant slices with tomato. Grate the tomato, add olive oil, add oregano, pepper and salt to taste. Put the tomato mix on top of a slice of eggplant and put in the oven for 15 minutes at 350 degrees F.
4. Yogurt. Preferably without sugar.
5. Any type of fruit is allowed.

After this ten-day diet you can incorporate a protein, preferably fish. Eat this protein once a week. You must incorporate foods such as spinach, brussels sprouts and eggplant that provide a variety of vitamins to your diet.

Try to continue the diet for 20 more days with all the dietary recommendations and the partial fasting. This will be combined with the simple exercise routine that I recommend in the following chapter.

For more delicious recipes visit my YouTube channel: *Nora Veronica Reynoso.*

16.

WORKING OUT TO LOVE YOUR BODY

THE 20 DAY ROUTINE

The following plan was designed for people who consider themselves beginners in completing a continuous 30 minute exercise routine. The objective is for to adapt the body so that it can withstand a more complex workout.

As the dict, this workout routine is simple and can be realized at home. The number of repetitions depend on your goal. You don't have to worry if you can't complete the routine on the first day. The goal is to get accustomed to a routine and that you can feel the benefits of exercise in only ten days.

Remember, if you have physical limitations of any kind to complete this workout you have to consult with your doctor first.

All the exercises described in this chapter can be found in my YouTube channel: *Nora Veronica Reynoso*.

WARM-UP EXERCISES

Warming up is vital and it's a great way to slowly increase your heart rate before doing any exercise routine. You should try to spend 10 to 15 minutes warming up so that your joints and your muscles can adjust and do the exercises.

Next up is a series of movements you should perform before starting your routine. Perform each movement, in order, for 60 seconds, without any rests in between. You should repeat each movement five times. Doing so will reduce the likelihood of injury, improve performance and make exercise more fun. Enjoy!

1. Head Movements
- Turn your head from side to side as if you were saying no. Do it gently and try touching your shoulders with your chin.
- Then move your head up and down, as if saying yes.
- Then bend your neck trying to make your right ear touch your right shoulder. Repeat with your left ear.

2. Arms and back
- Start by putting the palms of your hands on your head, then stretch your arms as high as possible and stay in that position for about 5 seconds.

3. Shoulders
- Clasp your hands behind your back and try to pull them over your lower back. Stretch your arms and move your shoulders back as far as you can, keep your arms raised and steady for five seconds.

4. Wrists and ankles
- Extend your arms in front of you and then draw circles with your wrists clockwise and then counterclockwise.
- Sitting on the floor or on a bench with your next extended, try to perform the same movement with your ankles.

5. Legs
- Standing with your legs parallel to your shoulders, try to perform a half-squat. Because this is just a warm up you should not lower yourself completely, and try to focus on your form.

FOUR EXERCISES FOR BEGINNERS

This is a four exercise routine for beginners, or for those who don't have an established routine. It must be performed at least for twenty straight days. Try to do three series for each exercise, with each series made up of twelve repetitions. You can rest for thirty seconds up to a minute in between series.

The following four-workout routine is for beginners, or people who do not have an established habit. It must be done at least 20 days in a row.

Three series have to be made for each exercise. Each series has 12 repetitions. Between each series you can take a break from thirty seconds to a minute.

1. Standing Crunches
- Stand with you feet shoulder width apart, shoulders down, and your arms overhead. Bring your right elbow to meet your left knee as you twist your waist, then return to the starting position and repeat on the opposite side. Focus on using your core, not your quads, to lift your knee and try to squeeze your obliques throughout. Continue to alternate sides for 60 seconds.

2. Squats
- Stand with your feet slightly wider than your hips, toes facing forward. Look straight ahead, with your arms out in front of your body. With your chest out, shoulders back, and abs tight, slowly lower your butt down as far as you can. Make sure your knees do not push forward past your toes. Return to starting position, without rounding your back as you stand. Try to complete fifteen to 20 repetitions.

- Squats are the best strength training exercises for beginners.

3. Alternating Lunges
- Stand up with your feet hip-width apart. Place your hands on your hips with your shoulders back and relaxed, and your chin up. Lunge forward with your right leg, then bend both knees and lower your hips until both knees are bent at a 90 degree angle.
- Rise and pull back the right leg to the starting position. Lunge forward with your left leg and keep alternating legs after each rep. Keep the torso upright all the time and make sure your knee doesn't extend past the toes when you lunge forward.
- This exercise tones the thighs, calves, butt and core. In fact, if you want to lose belly fat, forget doing crunches, lunges are the way to go.

4. Wall Push-Ups
- Face a wall, standing 4 inches farther than your arm's length and with your feet shoulder-width apart. Lean your body forward and put your palms flat against the wall at shoulder height and shoulder-width apart. Bring your chest to the wall and get as close as you can. Keep your feet flat on the floor. Hold the position for 1 second.

- Breathe out and slowly push yourself back until your arms are straight.
- These push-ups will strengthen your arms, shoulders, and chest. Try this exercise during a TV commercial break.
- Repeat 10 to 15 times.

Visit my YouTube channel: *Nora Veronica Reynoso*. You'll be able to see many more routines to help you get back in shape.

17.

THE SPECIAL INGREDIENT

IF YOU ARE READY to take on this challenge I only have to remind you that neither fasting, nor the strictest diet, nor long sessions at the gym will work if you don't do it with love. It sounds cheesy but loving oneself is the missing ingredient in our journey to rescue ourselves. I learned that we have to become our own lifeline. Problems will always be there trying to harm our bodies and our minds, but in that moment the only thing we can do is try to move forward, to meet new challenges and to live with one purpose in mind: Loving our life.

When we truly love the fact of being alive we start to pay attention to what we eat and what we drink without this ever becoming a sacrifice. Loving our body can also be done exercising. If this marvelous machine is well taken care of it will accomplish everything without a hitch. We will then be able to focus our energy in strengthening our mind and soul.

I invite you to discover your body's capacity to heal, to regenerate itself, and to live in harmony. I hope that one day, just as I did, you can say:

"Today I am rescuing myself!"

"Dare to look at yourself in the mirror knowing you did your best, and that tomorrow will always be a better day."

Photo by: Edward G Negron, 2018.

Made in the USA
Columbia, SC
31 August 2024

40858541R00087